Strategy

Strategy

The Art and Science of
Strategy Creation and Execution

STUART CRAINER + DES DEARLOVE

New York Chicago San Francisco Athens London Madrid
Mexico City Milan New Delhi Singapore Sydney Toronto

1 2 3 4 5 6 7 8 9 0   DOC/DOC   1 9 8 7 6 5 4 3

ISBN   978-0-07-182786-7
MHID   0-07-182786-2

e-ISBN 978-0-07-182754-6
e-MHID   0-07-182754-4

Library of Congress Cataloging-in-Publication Data
Crainer, Stuart.
   Thinkers50 strategy : the art and science of strategy creation and execution / by Stuart Crainer and Des Dearlove.
      pages cm
   Includes index.
   ISBN 978-0-07-182786-7 (pbk.) — ISBN 0-07-182786-2 (pbk.)
   1. Strategic planning. 2. Management. I. Dearlove, Des. II. Title.
   HD30.28.C723 2014
   658.4'012—dc23
                                                    2013031459

McGraw-Hill Education books are available at special quantity discounts to use as premiums and sales promotions or for use in corporate training programs. To contact a representative, please visit the Contact Us pages at www.mhprofessional.com.

Contents

Introduction

Strategy lies at the intersection of two important phenomena: the professionalization of management and the all too human desire for leaders and organizations to know where they are going and what the future may hold.

Over the last century we have seen management emerge as a profession. Bigger companies producing bigger quantities required a new breed of professionals. The visible hand of management was required to coordinate the flow of products to customers more efficiently than could Adam Smith's invisible hand.

From the beginning of this process it has been clear that planning is one of a manager's core activities. This was first expressed by the French thinker Henri Fayol early in the twentieth century. "To manage is to forecast and plan, to organize, to command, to co-ordinate and to control," is how Fayol pithily summarized the issue.

Forecasting and planning became subsumed into strategic management, and strategy remains one of the most vital ingredients in what managers actually do. Even in our tumultuous times, strategy is central to management. If we are in a competitive jungle, strategy allows us to figure a way out.

In this book we have gathered the major concepts that define our modern-day understanding of strategy and will introduce the thinkers we have talked to over the last 20 years, the thinkers behind those concepts, from Henry Mintzberg to Rita McGrath, Richard D'Aveni, and Roger Martin. The result is proof that strategy is alive and well and that the debate about the best ways forward remains as engagingly robust as ever.

Stuart Crainer and Des Dearlove
Thinkers50 Founders

CHAPTER

1

How We Got Here

Everyone in business is eager—sometimes desperate—to find an edge, a way to outmaneuver his or her rivals and secure sustainable long-term profits. This is where strategy comes in. A strategy is a plan or a pattern of actions that organizes the activities of a firm to meet its objectives. In doing so, strategy takes the resources of the firm and the external environment it operates in into account. In the case of a company, the overall strategic objective is primarily to attain competitive advantage, the more long-term, the better.

For organizations and strategy theorists, there are different forms of strategy. Corporate strategy is concerned with the strategy of the overall organization, its mix of businesses, and

1

the direction of the business and may be expressly articulated in vision and mission statements. Whereas business strategy concerns the individual business lines or units in a company, strategic management assesses internal strengths and weaknesses, external threats and opportunities, and the creation and implementation of strategies that link the two to the advantage of the company.

Today, strategy taxes the minds of executives (and governments) the world over as they weigh the forces railed against them, position their firms in markets, rally their resources, boost their capabilities, swim through blue and red oceans, and do their best to secure long-term survival. In the fast-paced global economy, there are a bewildering myriad of approaches to and views on strategy and what can make one company better than another.

Costas Markides, the charismatic London Business School professor and one of the most accessible thinkers on strategy, provides this overview:

> There is general agreement that every company needs a strategy—either explicit or implicit. Yet, there is surprisingly little agreement as to what strategy really is. Within both business and academic circles, it is not easy to identify two people who share the same definition of "strategy." Differences in opinion on the content and process of developing strategy are passionately argued. Yet these debates cease to matter when we realize two important points. First, strategy needs to be approached from a variety of perspectives. Second, rather than adopt a single perspective at the expense of all others, good strategies have to achieve a fine balance between seemingly divergent views.

What issues should senior executives consider in thinking about a new strategy and how should they think about them? Despite the apparent simplicity of this question, it is one of the most controversial in the field of management. As with most academic debates, when one probes below the surface, the apparently divergent points of view are in fact amazingly similar. Rather than depend on one perspective at the expense of all others, good strategies encompass elements from all the different perspectives and points of view.

When it comes to strategy, I have found that there are three problem areas of controversy. I believe that sound strategic thinking achieves a fine balance between the arguments surrounding: (1) what constitutes the content and process of strategy, (2) strategy as analysis or creativity and (3) strategy dynamics. Analyzing each area in turn will help in achieving that fine balance.

For example, consider the numerous ways that academics have defined strategy over the years—as positioning the company in its industry environment, as a collection of a few simple rules, as hustle, as stretch and leverage, as the embodiment of a company's values, and so on. It's easy to understand why even the *Economist* has claimed that "nobody really knows what strategy is."

Similar confusion and disagreements also exist around the process by which good strategies are developed. Let us first consider the debate on the content of strategy. Beyond the rhetoric, we can identify two main schools of thought on what strategy is.

The more "Porterian" (in reference to Michael Porter's work) view of strategy emphasizes the positioning elements. This school views strategy primarily as positioning the company in its industry environment. This is another way of saying that strategy is all about choosing a good game to play. The other main school of thought considers positioning to be static and old news. Proponents of this school encourage us to embrace the new and more dynamic view of strategy, which emphasizes outplaying and outmaneuvering competitors, no matter what game they are playing. According to this way of thinking, strategy is more about how you play the game than about choosing what game to play.

Strategy is both of these things: strategy must decide what game we want to play and then determine how to play that game well. As practised today, strategy is preoccupied with fixing the problems in the existing business rather than thinking about future businesses. The essence of a good strategy is to create new markets, new products and new industries. This leads to the position that strategy should be about competing for the industries of the future rather than competing for market share in the industries of today. It is hard to argue with the need to focus the organization's attention on discovering new markets. But this should not come at the expense of today's businesses.

Therefore, the key question for any company is not whether it should try to create the industries of the future but how to take care of its existing business while *at the same time* attempting to create the industries of the future. Every company should also prepare for an unknown future—either by trying to create this new future itself or by creating the conditions that would allow it to exploit the future when it unfolds.[1]

Similar fundamental concerns were expressed by Bain & Company's Chris Zook when we spoke:

It's interesting. I looked at a database recently of 300,000 employee surveys that were done with companies headquartered in Europe, and one question that was asked was, Do you have any idea what the company strategy is, what its priorities are, and what makes it special? And only two of five employees in the average business say they have any idea what that is. If you had a marching band or a football team where only two out of five knew the formation, that would be a problem, yet in the very best businesses, 85 percent of people say they really have an idea of what the business stands for. Whether it's a company like Nike that just jumps out at you as being about performance or Tetra Pak where it jumps out at you being it's about the packaging, so often having a really simple and clear and powerful differentiation is the essence of it.

And very often, in the crush of daily pressure and life, executives and management teams find their time frittered away and spent by everything that comes up, every daily crisis, and this is even more true today, with the speed at which the world is changing. And so I think that the essence is that it's very hard to be really self-aware of what are the very few things that you are excellent at.[2]

Military Strategy

As Markides and Zook suggest, strategy is a multifaceted and sometimes confusing part of any executive's life. Before we explore some of the contemporary takes on strategy, let's rewind. The word *strategy* derives from *strategia*, the Greek term for generalship, and the earliest studies of strategy were done by military commanders. Even today business executives and academics are fond of drawing on the work of military strategists. It is easy to see why when a predominantly capitalist, free market economy–driven world has promoted a mentality of win at all costs, defeat your rivals, and emerge victorious.

Strategic plans are couched in warlike notions. They exhort companies to seize competitive advantage, battle over market share, and struggle for differentiation. The trouble is that if the opposing army is doing the exact same thing, such strategies often cancel each other out or trigger immediate tit-for-tat retaliation. Strategy quickly reverts to tactical opportunism. As the German Field Marshal Helmuth Carl Bernard von Moltke memorably observed, "No battle plan ever survives contact with the enemy."[3]

Perhaps the most celebrated work from a military strategist is Sun Tzu's *The Art of War*, written several hundred years before BC slipped into AD and 2,500 years or so before executives started hiring strategy consultants. The book's actual title is *Sun Tzu Ping Fa*, which can be literally translated as "The Military Method of Venerable Mr. Sun."

A mainstay of bestselling business book lists, *The Art of War* is a feast of pithy, insightful aphorisms on strategy and tactics. "Deploy forces to defend the strategic points; exercise vigilance in preparation, do not be indolent," writes Sun Tzu. "Deeply investigate the true situation, secretly await their laxity. Wait until they leave their strongholds, then seize what they love."[4] It is required reading for mergers and acquisitions advisors everywhere.

Not that *The Art of War* is all brute force and brutality. There is stealth and cunning too. "If you are near the enemy, make him believe you are far from him. If you are far from the enemy, make him believe you are near," Sun Tzu advises. "To subdue the enemy's forces without fighting is the summit of skill. The best approach is to attack the other side's strategy; next best is to attack his alliances; next best is to attack his soldiers; the worst is to attack cities."[5]

The authorship of *The Art of War* remains uncertain. One suggestion is that it was authored by Sun Wu, a military general alive around 500 BC. The book is reputed to have led to a meeting between Sun Wu and his monarch, King Ho-lü of Wu. Sun Wu, unable to source a flipchart, apparently argued his case for military discipline by decapitating two of the king's concubines. Today's strategy consultants use less violent methods but are still likely to get an audience at the very top of the organization, so revered is the field of strategy and people who might provide advantageous insights. To many in the business world, strategy formulation remains the pinnacle of corporate endeavor.

Military Exercise

Right next to Sun Tzu's masterpiece, the bookshelf perusers in the strategy section are likely to find a number of other strategy books with a military association, such as B. H. Liddell-Hart's *Strategy* (1967), Miyamoto Mushashi's *A Book of Five Rings* (1974), and *The Prince* by Niccolò Machiavelli (1469–1527), a Renaissance masterpiece of cunning, intrigue, and brutal opportunism. Machiavelli, a Florentine diplomat, certainly understood the perils of being the first mover in a market, for example. "It ought to be remembered that there is nothing more difficult to take in hand, more perilous to conduct, or more uncertain in its success, than to take the lead in the introduction of a new order of things,"[6] he noted.

It was another soldier, Carl von Clausewitz (1780–1831), who emphasized the difference between strategy—the overall plan—and tactics—the planning of a discrete part of the overall plan, such as the battle. Von Clausewitz also introduced the idea of overarching strategic objectives, which he labeled "grand strategy." The debate about what constitutes strategy and tactics rumbles on today.

Von Clausewitz was a Prussian general who fought in the Napoleonic Wars, including at Waterloo, after which he became director of the Prussian war college in 1818. His book *On War* was unfinished and was published posthumously in 1831. In it, Von Clausewitz was beginning to appreciate the value of drawing comparisons between the conduct of business and war. "Rather than comparing it [war] to art we could more accurately compare it to commerce, which is also a conflict of interests and activities; and it is still closer to politics, which in turn may be considered as a kind of commerce on a larger scale," he wrote in *On War*.[7]

The Birth of Strategic Management

Fast-forward 150 years or so and it was in the 1960s when managers discovered strategy and, under the guise of strategic management, identified it as an important subset of management. "It struck me that if you look at strategy as an intellectual construct, a framework, a set of ideas, it really didn't exist in a formal way much before the 1960s," observes Walter Kiechel in *The Lords of Strategy: The Secret History of the New Corporate World*.[8]

In terms of intellectual first mover advantage, Peter Drucker claimed to get there first. Drucker somewhat immodestly noted that his book *Managing for Results*, published in 1964, was the "first book ever on what we now call strategy." Drucker chalked up many intellectual firsts, but in reality, his book was preceded by the business historian Alfred Chandler's *Strategy and Structure* published in 1962 (and, as Henry Mintzberg notes in his book *The Rise and Fall of Strategic Planning*, also by a 1962 *Harvard Business Review* article, "The Anatomy of Corporate Planning").

The business historian Chandler (1918–2007) saw strategy as "the determination of the long-term goals and objectives of an enterprise, and the adoption of courses of action and the allocation of resources necessary for carrying out these goals." Chandler's view, much disputed later on, was that strategy comes before structure. Develop your strategy and then construct the appropriate organizational structure to achieve that strategy.

Future contributions from the strategy community suggest that the strategy process is somewhat fuzzier than Chandler described it. In Chandler's world companies would hatch flawless strategies and then manufacture structures and organizational maps to fit them. A closer look at corporate reality suggests that strategy and structure mix somewhat more haphazardly. Still, Chandler must be credited with drawing attention to the importance of the link between strategy and structure.

Then, while the rest of the world was discovering Jimi Hendrix, the Beatles, free love, and hallucinogenics, managers were wrestling with the next developments in strategy, in particular the book *Corporate Strategy*, written by Igor Ansoff (1918–2002) and published in 1965.

When we interviewed Ansoff in the late 1980s, he told colorful stories about his birth in Vladivostock to a "400 percent" Russian mother and an American diplomat father and how his career change from executive to academic was the result of a period of contemplation during which he grew a beard and consumed a case of whiskey. His theories were less colorful but highly influential. Ansoff, an engineer and mathematician by training, worked for the RAND Corporation after university and then for the Lockheed Corporation. Leaving industry in 1963, he joined Carnegie Mellon's Graduate School of Business Administration and subsequently taught at a number of universities. It was his experiences at Lockheed that inspired his first book, in which he examined the implications of what he had learned while at Lockheed, in particular that there was "a practical method for strategic decision making within a business firm" that could be applied by other managers in their own organizations.

The world, said Ansoff, was struggling to cope with relentless change (as it continues to do today). Managers were wrestling with a "deluge of technology, the dynamism of the worldwide changes in market structure, and the saturation of demand in many major United States industries." In the face of such relentless change, many companies needed to "continually survey the product-market environment" for new opportunities, as no business could "consider itself immune to threats of product obsolescence and saturation of demand."

What managers needed to do, Ansoff decided, was conduct more analysis. There were, he suggested, four different but standard types of decision: decisions regarding strategy, policy, programs, and standard operating procedures. Among these, strategic decisions demanded the most management attention and energy. "The end product of strategic decisions is deceptively simple; a combination of products and markets is selected for the firm. This combination is arrived at by the addition of new product-markets, divestment from some old ones, and expansion of the present position," Ansoff noted.[9]

Strategic management was "the part of management which develops a firm's future profit potential by assuring that it does business in markets which have the potential of satisfying its objectives; that it offers products/services which these markets want; and that it offers them in a way which assures it a competitive advantage." This was opposed to operating management, which was "the part of management which, using the profit potential, optimizes a firm's profitability through efficient production, distribution and marketing its products/services generated by strategic management."[10]

To help with the strategic type of decision making, Ansoff offered the Ansoff model of strategic planning, which focused on corporate expansion and diversification rather than strategic planning overall. It was also analysis-heavy, and a common criticism of the overly analytical approach to strategic management was that it led to "paralysis by analysis," in which a lot of time was spent on the analysis of the data that such strategic plans were founded on, so much so that the plans were made but rarely implemented.

The association of Ansoff with paralysis by analysis is unfortunate. Actually, in response he moved on to develop a broader theory of strategic management. These ideas were strongly rooted in the importance of the environment and the belief that an organization needs to respond appropriately to the environment in which it operates. "In order to maximize return on investment, the aggressiveness of the firm's strategies and the responsiveness of the firm's management capabilities must match the turbulence of the environment," said Ansoff.[11] This at least has the ring of twenty-first-century reality.

There was no universal success formula for all firms, asserted Ansoff. The level of turbulence in the environment determines the strategy to be deployed for success. How aggressive that strategy is depends on the level of turbulence; the two must be aligned. Equally, the firm's management capability should be aligned with the environment. Finally, Ansoff indicated that the key internal capability variables that jointly determine a firm's success are cognitive, psychological, sociological, political, and anthropological.

When we asked Ansoff about his contribution, he replied as follows:

> First, I would like to be known as one of the first to bring a multidisciplinary approach to both exploratory theory and practical tools for helping environment-serving organizations succeed in turbulent environments.
>
> Second, I would like to be recognized as one of the first to offer a scientific proof that the age of universal prescriptions (like "stick to your strategic knitting" or "return to basics") is over; that the solution depends on the characteristics of the organization's environment; that each organization needs to diagnose its future environment and then devise its own appropriate solutions; and that I contributed a practical tool for matching a firm to its environment.

The Smartest People in the Room

In the early development of strategic management theory, consulting firms played an important role. Although theories of strategy differ widely, most have at least one thing in common: the use of a diagram or model, often the ubiquitous matrix. Yet before the 1960s, models were largely the playthings of economists. In the 1960s, however, one management consulting firm in particular popularized the use of models in strategic management.

The Australian Bruce Henderson (1915–1992) was an engineer who eventually found his way into the strategic planning department at General Electric. In *The Lords of Strategy*, Walter Kiechel describes Henderson as "extraordinarily, impossibly difficult but, at the same time, creative, just a fascinating guy."[12] After leaving GE, Henderson joined the management consultancy Arthur D. Little before setting up his own consultancy, the Boston Consulting Group (BCG).

One of the first, possibly the first, pure strategy consultancy, BCG soon established itself. One of its earliest strategy models was the experience curve. The origins of the model go back to the idea of the learning curve associated with a company called Curtiss Aircraft in the 1920s. Henderson modified the idea and extended it to strategy rather than manufacturing. He coined the term *experience curve*, which described the relationship between unit costs, cumulative production, and experience. As cumulative production increases, productivity costs decline. Why? Because the more often workers repeat processes, the better they get at doing their jobs, the more efficient the organization becomes, and the faster the company gets competitive advantage.

The concept came from observations of growth rates in the semiconductor industry in the 1960s. Using price data from the Electronic Industries Association, the researchers detected two patterns. In one, prices remained constant for long periods before steeply declining over a long period; in the other, prices declined at a constant rate of some 25 percent each time accumulated experience doubled. This was dubbed the experience curve.

BCG went on to develop a tool kit of strategy concepts that included sustainable growth, time-based competition, segment-of-one marketing, value-based strategy, and total shareholder value. The model that the firm is best known for, however, is the Boston matrix, which measures market growth and relative market share for all the businesses in a particular firm, making it easier to know which are worth investing in and which are likely to be a waste of time and money.

When mapped onto a two-by-two matrix, measuring market share and growth rate, a portfolio of companies can be sorted into four types. They are either cash cows, dull, safe, and highly profitable cash generators that need frequent milking; dogs with low market share and low growth, possibly needing rehoming; stars, stratospheric, with high growth and high market share; and the risky question marks (or wildcats in some versions), where there is high growth and low market share.

From the business perspective the Boston matrix was a great model: accessible, simple, and useful. But it was also limited, reducing the competitive business world to two measures of success—growth and profitability—a view that held sway for decades afterward and still does to an extent. It encouraged a preoccupation with market share.

But behind the smart strategy models was an even smarter business model. Bruce Henderson set up the model of the consulting firm as hugely competitive and stocked with the world's best brains. One of his recruits was Peter Lampl, now Sir Peter, founder of the Sutton Trust. "When I joined BCG, it was the best management consulting firm in the world. I was the first person to join BCG in Boston directly from a European business school. And I was treated like dirt! It had a total free market system. So I arrived at BCG in 1973. I didn't know anyone. They said, 'There's your desk.' And I said, 'Well, what do I do?' I was told that I had to find work, I had to talk to managers and vice presidents and get them to employ me. I had a pretty tough start," Lampl told us. "The whole measure of performance at

BCG was billability: how many hours you bill clients each week. That's all that mattered. Bruce Henderson had a chart up in the office where everyone's monthly billability was listed, as well as their moving annual billability, so you could see every month how everybody was doing. If people were declining in billability, they would disappear. All of a sudden, they wouldn't show up. There was a huge churn rate, a half-life of about two and a half years. Bruce believed in survival of the fittest. It was crazy but unbelievably exciting. At that time BCG was leading the pack. We were developing portfolio strategy, the experience curve, and so on. We had some wonderful assignments."

Other consulting firms were also on the lookout for persuasive strategy models. McKinsey already had its critical success factors, an early 1960s nod to the resource-based strategy and core competencies school of thought that would emerge in the 1980s. Then, through its work with GE, it developed the grandly titled General Electric and McKinsey Factor Portfolio Matrix. Companies were scored along two dimensions, one composed of nine industry attractiveness measures and the other composed of 12 internal business strength measures.

The New Era of Strategy

So far, so analytical. These early steps in the strategy field paved the way for the explosion in interest that followed. With corporations hooked on the notion that it was possible to achieve the seemingly impossible—long-term competitive advantage over one's rivals—they were eager consumers of the torrent of material on strategic management that emerged over the next decades.

The next big breakthrough was led by Harvard Business School's Michael Porter (see Chapter 2), who translated an industrial economics framework into a business strategy context. Porter was big on seriousness and rationality. "His work is academic almost to a fault," observed the *Economist*. "Mr Porter is about as likely to produce a blockbuster full of anecdotes and boosterish catch-phrases as he is to deliver a lecture dressed in bra and stockings."[13] He still is.

Highly researched and determinedly logical, Porter linked success to market positioning. He ground down the competitive environment into five forces that firms should attend to and offered some thoughts about how firms might use an assessment of those five forces to adopt a strategy that would secure better commercial advantage. Porter also introduced the notion of the value chain, a common business concept today.

Porter's approach to strategy was decidedly analytical, founded on data and information gathering. In Porter's writing, people are generally conspicuous by their absence. Even so, Porter dominated the strategy theory landscape during the 1980s, and it was not until the late 1980s and early 1990s that a major new school of thought began to gain traction: the resource-based view of strategy.

There was an early glimmer of the resource-based approach in the work of the economists Edith Penrose and Birger Wernerfelt. However, it took two business school academics, C. K. Prahalad and Gary Hamel, to formulate and popularize the resource-based view of strategy for a wider business audience. Strategic positioning was inadequate, Prahalad and Hamel argued. Competitive advantage came from within, not from a detailed analysis of markets and some subsequent maneuvering based on that analysis. What was really important, they said, was a company's core competencies. Every company had its core competencies. It was just a question of working out exactly what those core competencies were and then building and utilizing them to the best advantage.

If Porter's work was an incremental but nevertheless significant shift from static strategic planning, Prahalad's and Hamel's championing of core competencies was a big breakthrough. The challenge to the strategic positioning and data and analysis paradigm made the strategy field more attractive to innovative thinkers. Not that data and analysis disappeared. Far from it; witness the recent interest in the power of big data. It was more the case that data and analysis became the tools of strategists rather than an end in themselves.

What followed was a dramatic increase from both consultants and academics in strategic theories and tools. Work by existing theorists gained wider recognition, and new names became visible. Richard D'Aveni devised strategies appropriate for a fast-changing world of hypercompetition (see Chapter 4). Henry Mintzberg speculated about the strategy process itself and how strategy was formed (see Chapter 6). W. Chan Kim and Renée Mauborgne pondered the challenges faced by corporations swimming in what they described as red oceans and showed them how to chart a course to more temperate blue oceans (see Chapter 5). Most recently we have seen Rita McGrath convincingly sounding the death knell for competitive advantage (see Chapter 2) and Chris Zook recounting the challenges for corporations venturing beyond their core (see Chapter 3).

Thinkers have applied their minds to considering how strategy implementation works best and the practice of strategy. Roger Martin and P&G CEO A. G. Lafley explore strategy in action in their book *Playing to Win* (see Chapter 6), and strategy guru Richard Rumelt considers the highs and lows of strategy practice in his book *Good Strategy/Bad Strategy.*

Strategy has strayed off the corporate path. Increasingly, politics touches the lives of business leaders. Strategy thinkers such as David Baron and David Bach have explored the byways of nonmarket strategy, bringing it back to its impact on the success of organizations in meeting their objectives (see Chapter 7).

Finally, strategy has returned full circle to its ancient roots, being analyzed in the context of governments and nations. This time, however, instead of strategy being applied to military conflict, it is applied to the struggle for economic power and prosperity. Thus, Porter, Hamel, D'Aveni, Pankaj Ghemawat, and others have considered the competitive strategy of nations and political and economic systems (see Chapter 8). The world is strategic.

What are the implications for managers? That is less clear. In fact, corporate strategy is currently experiencing another of its periodic crises of confidence.

As the Columbia professor Rita McGrath told us: "Strategy is really struggling both in the field and in the real world. You are seeing a bit of a gap. Porter's five forces, the BCG matrix, SWOT [strengths, weaknesses, opportunities, and threats] analysis, a lot of those tools came from an era when competition was much less vigorous. They are great tools in the context in which they were developed. If you've got a stable industry structure and you've got things that you can actually measure, they still work. But today we're seeing industries competing with industries, different arenas where competition manifests itself. Strategy, entrepreneurship, and innovation are all bleeding into each other."

And as they bleed into each other, we are witnessing the emergence of new ideas about and models of strategy.

CHAPTER 2

Understanding Competitive Advantage

What makes some companies successful while apparently similar companies fail? How do you achieve long-term success? In the 1970s these were questions that taxed corporate executives, yet no one had a persuasive or authoritative answer. In the past, technological innovation—mastering mass production, for example—management science, exemplary leadership, and rearrangement of organizational structures all conferred temporary advantage on companies. Yet there was no systematic decoding of the strategies that delivered competitive success.

In the 1960s strategists were predominantly planners, attempting to map out routes to a prosperous future, often many years ahead. Igor Ansoff and a small number of other academics, in addition to the burgeoning management consulting industry, were pointing to a different role for the strategist. But it took a professor from Harvard Business School using research data and detailed analysis and applying forensic logic to his subject to change the way companies viewed (and still view) strategy. Applied correctly, strategy could provide a framework for understanding the world organizations competed in, allowing them to fashion a successful future.

That professor was Michael Porter. No one has had a bigger impact on modern business strategy than Porter. He casts a long shadow. It is telling that more than 40 years after he published his five forces framework, every strategy theorist still positions his or her own work in relation to his. Porter is the starting point and the benchmark.

Porter was precociously talented and intellectually persuasive. Born in Ann Arbor, Michigan, in 1947, he was the son of an army officer. Much of his youth was spent moving around the world as his father had different postings. (Later on, Porter served with the U.S. Army Reserve, rising to the rank of captain.) Porter excelled both academically and at sports. He studied aerospace and mechanical engineering at Princeton for his first degree. He was also an all-state high school football and baseball player, played intercollegiate golf while at Princeton, and was named to the 1968 NCAA All-American golf team.

He might have chosen professional golf as a career but instead decided to continue his academic studies. At Harvard, Porter completed his MBA in 1971 and his doctorate in business economics in 1973. It was while he was working on his PhD that Porter was mentored by the economist Richard Caves, noted for his work on creative entrepreneurship. Porter became one of the youngest tenured professors at Harvard when he joined the faculty at the age of 26.

Feel the Force

It didn't take long for Porter to make his mark. In 1979 his article "How Competitive Forces Shape Strategy" appeared in the *Harvard Business Review*. This was followed by a longer exposition in his 1980 book *Competitive Strategy: Techniques for Analyzing Industries and Competitors*.

The timing was perfect. During the 1970s, Japanese companies had threatened the dominance of U.S. corporations, making significant inroads into the market share of American companies in many industries. The initial response to the success of Japanese companies was one of denial and disbelief; commentators argued that Japanese success was due to lower costs, notably lower labor costs. However, it was soon apparent that there were more fundamental forces at work.

In *Competitive Strategy* and again in *Competitive Advantage*, his next book, published in 1985, Porter introduced three central and linked concepts that underpinned his ideas about competition and competitive advantage. Significantly, Porter used the term *competitive strategy* to refer to creating competitive advantage in each of the various businesses in which a diversified company might compete. Corporate strategy concerned the question of what businesses a company should be in and how those different businesses should be managed.

These concepts formed the foundation of the competitive positioning approach to strategy. Strategy was concerned with a business obtaining the most advantageous position within an industry compared with rival businesses. "The essence of formulating competitive strategy is relating a company to its environment," Porter wrote. This focused and disciplined approach dominated strategy thinking throughout the 1980s.

The first of Porter's central ideas, still taught in business schools around the world, was developed from microeconomics, in particular an industrial economics framework known as the structure-conduct performance (SCP) paradigm. Porter translated this framework into the context of business strategy and created the strategy model that he remains best known for: the five forces framework.

In *Competitive Strategy*, Porter wrote, "In any industry, whether it is domestic or international or produces a product or a service, the rules of competition are embodied in five competitive forces."[1] Those five competitive forces are:

1. **Entry of new competitors.** New competitors necessitate a competitive response that will inevitably use some of your resources, thus reducing profits. Barriers to entry include economies of scale, product differentiation, government policies, and access to distribution channels.

2. **Threat of substitutes.** If there are viable alternatives to your product or service in the marketplace, the prices you can charge will be limited.

3. **Bargaining power of buyers.** If customers have bargaining power, they will use it. This will reduce profit margins and, as a result, affect profitability. A number of factors affect a buyer's bargaining power, including

degree of standardization, threat of backward integration, level of costs, and level of switching costs.

4. **Bargaining power of suppliers.** Given power over you, suppliers will increase their prices and adversely affect your profitability.

5. **Rivalry among existing competitors.** Competition leads to the need to invest in marketing, research and development (R&D), or price reductions, which will reduce your profits. Factors affecting this rivalry include the types of competitors, the nature of exit barriers, the amount of differentiation, and the minimum size of investment.

The five forces provided a framework that companies could use to better understand their industry and their competitive position within that industry. As Porter notes: "The collective strength of these five competitive forces determines the ability of firms in an industry to earn, on average, rates of return on investment in excess of the cost of capital. The strength of the five forces varies from industry to industry, and can change as an industry evolves."[2]

Understanding these forces that shape industry competition was soon regarded as the starting point for all those involved in formulating strategy. But what to do?

In the original *Harvard Business Review* article Porter identified three possible courses of action. Executives can position the company so that it is best placed to use its capabilities to defend itself against competitive forces. As Porter noted: "An effective competitive strategy takes offensive or defensive action in order to create a defendable position against the five competitive forces."[3]

Alternatively, it is possible to influence the balance of the forces through strategic moves and so improve the company's position. Or firms can anticipate shifts in the factors that underlie the forces and then choose a strategy appropriate for the new balance of forces, hoping to gain a competitive advantage before rivals manage to respond.

In *Competitive Strategy*, Porter also introduced the concept of generic strategies. These were generic strategic positions that companies needed to adopt: "viable approaches to dealing with . . . competitive forces," as Porter put it.[4]

The first was *differentiation*: competing on the basis of value added to customers (such as quality, service, or unique features) so that customers will pay a premium to cover higher costs.

The second was *cost-based leadership*: offering products or services at the lowest cost. This enables the firm to compete on price where required and, when it is not required, to make high levels of sustainable profits. Quality and service are not unimportant, but cost reduction provides focus to the organization. Cost leadership requires investment in current production technology and talented staff.

The third generic strategy relates to *focus* and the scope to which differentiation or cost-based leadership is deployed. "Sometimes the firm can successfully pursue more than one approach as its primary target, though this is rarely possible," said Porter. "Effectively implementing any of these generic strategies usually requires total commitment, and organizational arrangements are diluted if there's more than one primary target."

If a company failed to focus on any of the three generic strategies, it was liable to encounter problems, Porter asserted. "The firm failing to develop its strategy in at least one of the three directions—a firm that is stuck in the middle—is in an extremely poor strategic situation," Porter wrote. "The firm lacks the market share, capital investment, and resolve to play the low-cost game, the industry-wide differentiation necessary to obviate the need for a low-cost position, or the focus to create differentiation or low cost in a more limited sphere.

"The firm stuck in the middle is almost guaranteed low profitability. It either loses the high-volume customers who demand low prices or must bid away its profits to get this business away from low-cost firms. Yet it also loses high-margin businesses—the cream—to the firms who are focused on high-margin targets or have achieved differentiation overall. The firm stuck in the middle also probably suffers from a blurred corporate culture and a conflicting set of organizational arrangements and motivation system."[5]

The Value Chain

The third element of Porter's strategy triumvirate is the value chain and system. "Every firm is a collection of activities that are performed to design, produce, market, deliver, and support its product," Porter notes.

For Porter, competitive advantage is connected to the way a company organizes its activities. Porter used a systems-based approach to break down the analysis of the activities of the firm and the way a firm uses those activities to create value. Value, said Porter, is derived from the company using the resources at its disposal to transform inputs into outputs that customers will buy.

People choose to eat in restaurants for a variety of reasons. They could buy the ingredients and cook a meal at home.

A restaurant, however, creates value by taking inputs, such as the raw ingredients, and using its resources, such as the chef, to create an output, the meal, which the diner eats. For the business this creates value through the way it conducts and arranges its activities. The consumers buy value by comparing the products and services of various competing firms.

Porter divides value activities into two categories. There are the primary activities that add value directly. These include inbound and outbound logistics—storing and distributing the inputs of product or service and storing and distributing the finished products and services; operations—transforming inputs into the final product or service; marketing and sales; and service—enhancing and maintaining the value of the product. In addition, support activities—procurement, technology development, human resource management, and infrastructure—indirectly add value.

Together these three ideas provided the perfect strategic arsenal for management. A company uses its analysis of the five forces to assess the potential profitability of an industry and its competitive position within that industry to evaluate the likelihood of new entrants and substitute products, the power of customers and suppliers, and the threat of new rivals.

Having completed a five forces analysis, organizations can opt for one of Porter's two main generic strategies. They can go for a differentiation strategy, with the objective of charging customers a premium price for goods on the basis that the customers perceive the particular product or service to be sufficiently superior to others. Alternatively, they can go for a low-cost strategy and be the cheapest in the market.

Finally, it is necessary to make sure that the value chain—that is, all the activities that contribute to the final value of the products and services—supports the firm's generic strategy.

The Great Debate

Porter's exposition of strategic positioning became the strategy method du jour during the 1980s and was adopted by many corporations large and small. It offered the attraction of being more dynamic and proactive than strategic planning and provided the comforting reassurance of being supported by reams of data and deep analysis of the competitive environment.

Porter's model is probably the one most taught in business history. To this day it remains a staple in every MBA program. Generations of students have absorbed its wisdom. But as time passed, there emerged the nagging suspicion that strategic positioning did not provide the whole strategy picture, that it was not the blueprint for competitive domination that so many executives yearned for, and that in its focus on markets it discounted the contribution of internal factors, such as employee knowledge, interfirm relationships, and many other aspects of organizational life, to competitive success.

Among the most perceptive critics of Porter's approach is Richard D'Aveni (see Chapter 4). We asked D'Aveni about the difference between the way he thought about strategy and Michael Porter's perspective on the subject.

It's vastly different. Porter's model from his 1980 book is about the creation of an oligopolistic industry, one in which all the players cooperate and build barriers to entry so that they keep out companies that are unfriendly. And then inside the barriers they build friendly companies that divide up the marketplace and collude on price, though, of course, they do that all through signals rather than explicitly.

Porter talks about the deescalation of rivalry in an industry to increase margins. What I like to talk about is the use of even price wars to create growth. So you change your margins by lowering them, create shareholder value by creating more rapid growth, and rather than living in peace with each other, you actively disrupt each other's core competency. You attempt to obsolete the leader's core competency, and when you do that, you become the new leader.

In Porter, thanks to barriers to entry, there are a few industry leaders and they're unchallengeable so that you are left with a peripheral market. If we followed Porter's model, all we would have is a world of people predescribed in a caste system, a world of corporations stuck in their caste. And the greatest companies don't see the barriers there.

I'll give you a very simple example, Toyota versus General Motors. General Motors spent years and years building up a service dealer network. Eventually, it had between 6,000 and 7,000 service dealers and spent billions on supporting those franchisees or dealerships. Then Toyota shows up and simply makes a car that needs much less service. And all of those billions are sunk costs and wasted and actually work against you.

Differentiation as a strategy is overrated. Because you have to really change an industry structure to deal with the problems we see in today's world, especially when it comes to commoditization, which is a black plague on modern corporations, a deadly disease that's spreading like crazy.

New Takes on Competitive Advantage

Others are also taking aim at the central premise of Porterian strategic logic. Rita McGrath is a professor at the Columbia University Graduate School of Business in New York and an expert on strategic business growth in uncertain environments. Like D'Aveni, she argues that the days of sustainable competitive advantage are numbered.

McGrath is the author or coauthor (with Ian MacMillan) of three books: *The Entrepreneurial Mindset: Strategies for Continuously Creating Opportunity in an Age of Uncertainty* (2000), *Market Busters: Forty Strategic Moves That Fuel Exceptional Business Growth* (2005), and *Discovery-Driven Growth: A Breakthrough Process to Reduce Risk and Seize Opportunity* (2009). Her most recent book is *The End of Competitive Advantage: How to Keep Your Strategy Moving as Fast as Your Business* (2013).

In *Discovery-Driven Growth*, McGrath explores how businesses can pursue dynamic growth and encourage innovative new ventures without jeopardizing the enterprise through undue risk taking. She provides tools and processes to allow businesses to exploit their opportunities. In *The End of Competitive Advantage*, she goes further.

The book begins with a candid assessment of the state of strategy, something we asked her about.

At the start of the book you say that strategy is stuck. Explain.

Well, if you think about the models and frameworks that had an impact on the field in the last 20 or 30 years, what's really new? We've had a lot of reliance on frameworks from the past that worked for a different era. I can't think of anything that's really had a big impact in the last 20 years. And I think that's because we're still looking for this mythical thing called a sustainable competitive advantage, and if you can't find one of those, then what do you do?

Two of the fundamental assumptions of strategy makers are that industry matters most and that strategy is about searching for competitive advantage, and when we find it, it will be sustainable. You say both of those things are up in the air. Can you explain?

I think it's important to note that industry isn't the major issue anymore. If you go back to the days of the corn wet milling case, you were competing to be in a relative market share game with other competitors in your industry. Today, what we're seeing is that it's actually industry-to-industry competition. So an example that I like to use is that today spending on communications and iPhones and other gadgets is actually eating away at the money that used to be spent on restaurants, on dining, on automotive, on travel. And so if you're a steakhouse, let's say, and you think you're competing with other steakhouses and that's how you're thinking about the world, you're going to be missing something very important.

And if competitive advantage is no longer sustainable, then we really are talking about redefining the whole nature of strategy, aren't we?
I think you're quite right. Getting rid of the sustainable concept does redefine the entire competitive landscape. And I think what we're going to see in the future is that firms that succeed over the long run are going to be really good at finding ideas, developing those ideas into business concepts, launching those business concepts, doing the exploitation thing, which is what strategy was always all about, but then also disengaging. And where I think firms need to change is to develop both the front end, the innovation incubation launch base, and the back end, the disengagement phase.

And so what you're going to be seeing is almost as though they're surfing through these waves of advantage. You'll have one wave come and then it goes away, another wave come and then it goes away. And firms that are good at surging competitive advantage are going to be okay with that.

So if the strategy landscape is really changing in the way you say, what does that mean for the old tools? What does that mean for Porter's five forces? What does it mean for the Boston matrix? After all, a whole generation of managers grew up using those tools.

You're absolutely right that a whole generation of managers did grow up with all those tools, five forces, Boston matrix, all those things, and they still work in the right boundary conditions. They still work when you're exploiting an advantage that's fairly easy to define and your major competition is other firms within that category.

Where I think those tools no longer work is the whole innovation phase and the disengagement phase. And if I were to name one place where those tools just don't have anything to say at all, it's what about disengagement, what about landline telephony or dial-up Internet or physical phone books? What do those tools have to say about those kinds of thing?

And there's been some work on exit and exit barriers and so forth, but we haven't really taken it on as a mainstream function of strategy. Similarly, we haven't really taken on innovation as a mainstream function of strategy. Strategy traditionally has been about that exploitation phase, where things are more stable. Now we have to think about what tools we use when things aren't so stable.

In the past we talked about barriers to entry, but it sounds as though what you're saying is that now

*we've got to start thinking in terms of barriers
to exit.*

Absolutely. That's a really smart comment, this notion
of barriers to exit. I argue that one of the things firms
are going to do differently is they're going to be
much more careful about sinking lots of assets and
lots of investment into specifically competitive places
because if you need to move fast, you don't want a lot
of fixed assets. You want to be able to use assets that
are fairly fungible. And one of the arguments I make
in the book is that it's access to assets rather than own-
ership of assets that we're going to see as the defining
issue in how you expend resources going forward.

*So if strategic advantage is no longer sustainable,
what should managers and leaders be doing? What's
the agenda for them?*

The difference in leadership behavior that you're
going to be seeing is an emphasis much more on
information traveling fast. So in the book I use the
example of Ford and Alan Mulally, CEO at Ford,
who basically said that you can't manage a secret. So
we're going to see a lot less of the management of
bring me the numbers, hit the goals, don't bring me
bad news, don't bring me a problem that you don't
have a solution to. That kind of management, which
works really well when things are stable, we're going
to see that going away.

We're going to see a lot more leadership that
involves influencing people and getting people

engaged. We're going to see much more candor, much more emphasis on being realistic, and also much more emphasis on keeping individuals and networks engaged, because in the past you used to be able to say a hierarchical reward was going to be the thing, so you start off at level 14 and you end up at level 2, and that's Nirvana. And I think we will see much less of that in how we manage careers in the future or how leaders engage people in the future.

You talk in the book about innovation proficiency. What is innovation proficiency, and how can companies achieve it?

Strategy and innovation, which used to be distinct activities, are blurring. When I started my professional career, innovation was over there, that weird thing that the creative people did, and strategy was over here and was all about positioning and markets and so forth. Now they're converging. So one of the things I argue that companies need to get better at is developing what I call innovation proficiency. And what that involves is having funds for it, having a governing mechanism for it, having people who actually do it for a living. It used to be innovation was always a great job but a lousy career.

What we're going to see now is companies actually building out that capability in a very systematic way. An example is the Australian logistics company Brambles, which has a really exciting business. They were founded on the basis of thousands of pallets left behind by the armored troops after World War II in Australia, and they get paid for shipping these pallets all around the world. Now, you wouldn't think a company like that would be a hotbed of innovation, yet they've really turned it into a systemic capability.

What they've realized is that one of the biggest barriers to innovation for a P&L [profit and loss] manager is the risk of trying something new that backfires. So, what do you do if it doesn't work? The worry is that it's going to show up in my numbers, it's going to make me look bad. So what the CEO has done is he's actually allocated funds in such a way that if the business succeeds, the P&L manager gets all the credit, but if it doesn't work out, corporate takes the hit. And so as a consequence, instead of the usual managers' response, which is, Oh, I don't want those innovation things, they're too risky, they're like, Bring it on, bring it on, give me as many as you can because it's only upside.

That's an example of the kind of thing that companies that are good at innovation do.

Let's be absolutely clear. We're not saying that competitive advantage isn't sustainable anywhere? There are still pockets of it in the economy. Is that right?
Yes, I would say there are still pockets of the economy where you can find the sustainable advantage. So if you take Rolls-Royce or Steinway pianos or something like that, they're niche businesses where the brand really matters or the customers are superloyal or busi-

nesses like Boeing where it's just really, really hard to build airplanes. So I still think there are places where you can find sustainable advantage, and the traditional tools I would say work pretty well in those places. But we have to grapple with the fact that less and less of the economy is represented by those kinds of industries, with those kinds of characteristics.

How are your ideas different from those of some of the other strategy thinkers? I'm thinking of Richard D'Aveni's notion of hypercompetition and Chan Kim and Renée Mauborgne's blue ocean strategy, in both cases talking about the transient nature of competitive advantage.

It's interesting to question whether what I'm writing about is really different from what's come before. And certainly we had Ian McMillan back in the 1980s talking about seizing strategic opportunity, Richard D'Aveni in the 1990s talking about hypercompetition. Certainly we've had blue ocean strategy, which I think was 2005. So I think all of us are seeing the same phenomena, except we're coming up with a different response to it.

The big difference in what I'm doing versus what's come before is to say, Okay, let's accept it. Once you've gotten over the shock and awe of oh my God, advantage has gone, how do we now develop strategies and develop companies that can manage this? I think we still have a lot of work to do here because if I look at how companies are actually run, not very many of them are actually run with this notion that strategy has got to change and that you've got less sustainable ways of operating.

So just as an example, typically we think about careers as steps up a ladder. And I think increasingly we're going to have to think of careers as—the popular word is *gigs*, or in a recent issue of the *Harvard Business Review* they're calling it *tours of duty*. So increasingly we're going to see people building careers that are maybe spanning multiple companies and may be spanning multiple experiences. They're not going to be all one kind of career anymore. And that has big implications for individuals for how you prepare. And so I think the big aha! to me is that we need to manage really differently if we accept this idea of nonsustainable advantage.

Does that mean that stability, which we used to assume was the norm, is now dangerous?

Yes, I would say stability is risky. By the time you need change management, it's almost too late. You want to be in continual motion. There are some things you want to keep stable as an organization. You want stability in values, you want stability in leadership, you want stability in your core reason for being. And in some of the work that underlies the book I actually found firms that were capable of supersuccess in this very dynamic environment and combined stability with motion. So they had a lot of stability in things like values and talent and networks and developing

people and incredible dynamism in investments and
locations, how they move people around. And so
it's this combination of stability with dynamism that
seems to be the trick.

CHAPTER 3

Getting to
the Core

By the end of 1980s, the strategic management world was in a rut. Strategic positioning went some way toward explaining the difference in performance of apparently similar companies in similar markets, yet there was something lacking. A large part of the puzzle was still unaccounted for. Instead of looking outward at the world from the organizations, strategists began to look inward, at the firm's resources. It was the beginning of a new phase: resource-based strategy.

Many people would eventually contribute to the development of the resource-based view of strategic management. Economists had already described firms as a set of resources, with Edith Penrose's work on the growth of the firm in the late

1950s and Birger Wernerfelt's "A Resource-Based View of the Firm" in 1984.[1]

Initially, though, it was two academics who met at the University of Michigan, Gary Hamel and C. K. Prahalad, whose work garnered the most attention. As Prahalad and Hamel observed, a change was needed if Western economies were to thrive and fend off the threat from Japan. "As 'strategy' has blossomed, the competitiveness of Western companies has withered. This may be coincidence, but we think not," they noted.

A graduate of Andrews University in Michigan, Hamel worked as a hospital administrator before completing his PhD in international business at the Ross School of Business at the University of Michigan. Hamel was a rapidly speaking enthusiast, a restless mustachioed strategy revolutionary. At Michigan, Hamel met his eventual mentor, Coimbatore Krishnao—C. K.—Prahalad.

Calm and deliberate, Prahalad (1941–2010) was a perfect sparring partner for Hamel. Prahalad was one of the first of several notable management academics from India whose rise to prominence reflected the growing global importance of the Indian economy. Prahalad was born in the state of Tamil Nadu in the town of Coimbatore and studied physics at the University of Madras (now Chennai) before joining the Union Carbide battery company as a manager. Prahalad traveled to the United States to continue his education, completing his doctorate at Harvard and teaching in both India and the United States before joining the business school faculty at the University of Michigan, where he was eventually appointed to the Harvey C. Fruehauf Chair of Business Administration.

As Hamel noted of his longtime collaborator: "We shared a deep dissatisfaction with the mechanistic way strategy was carried out."[2] In the mid-1980s the two established themselves at the vanguard of contemporary thinking on strategy, "separating the shit from the Shinola, the hype from the reality, and the timeless from the transient," as Hamel characteristically put it.

Strategic Intentions

In the early 1990s, many firms were struggling to stay in business. Cost cutting and widespread staff layoffs were the order of the day; business process reengineering was the latest management trend. Hamel and Prahalad felt that the discipline of management strategy was adopting increasingly limited perspectives. "Among the people who work on strategy in organizations and the theorists, a huge proportion, perhaps 95 percent, are economists and engineers who share a mechanistic view of strategy. Where are the theologists, the anthropologists to give broader and fresher insights?" they asked.

It was time for a new approach to corporate strategy. "By the 1990s strategy had become discredited," Hamel told us. "All too often 'vision' was ego masquerading as foresight; planning was formulaic, incrementalist, and largely a waste of time in a world of discontinuous change; 'strategic' investments were those that lost millions, if not billions, of dollars. As strategy professors, C.K. and I had a simple choice: change jobs or try to reinvent strategy for a new age. We chose the latter course."

Hamel and Prahalad began to reinvent strategy with two *Harvard Business Review* articles, "Strategic Intent" in 1989 and

"The Core Competence of the Corporation" in 1990, followed by the publication of their book *Competing for the Future* in 1994. In those publications they introduced and refined their concept of core: "the collective learning in the organization, especially how to coordinate diverse production skills and integrate multiple streams of technologies."[3]

In "Strategic Intent," Hamel and Prahalad note that the existing strategic paradigm misses some important factors: "Assessing the current tactical advantages of known competitors will not help you understand the resolution, stamina, or inventiveness of potential competitors." They quote Sun Tzu in support of their argument: "All men can see the tactics whereby I conquer," wrote Tzu, "but what none can see is the strategy out of which great victory is evolved."

The duo were dismissive of Western strategic thought. "It is not very comforting to think that the essence of Western strategic thought can be reduced to eight rules for excellence, seven Ss, five competitive forces, four product life-cycle stages, three generic strategies, and innumerable two-by-two matrices.

"Yet for the past 20 years, 'advances' in strategy have taken the form of ever more typologies, heuristics, and laundry lists, often with dubious empirical bases. Moreover, even reasonable concepts like the product life cycle, experience curve, product portfolios, and generic strategies often have toxic side effects: They reduce the number of strategic options management is willing to consider. They create a preference for selling businesses rather than defending them. They yield predictable strategies that rivals easily decode."[4]

Too frequently, say Hamel and Prahalad, strategy is "seen as a positioning exercise in which options are tested by how they fit the existing industry structure." But as the existing industry structure often reflects the strengths of the industry leader, this means that companies are invariably playing by the rules of the dominant companies in the industry, and that is usually "competitive suicide."

Hamel and Prahalad offer their own concept of strategic intent—an obsession with winning at all levels of the organization—and advocate using intent consistently to guide resource allocations. In doing so, organizations should set themselves a number of challenges: to create a sense of urgency, to develop a competitor focus at every level, to provide employees with the skills needed to work effectively, to give the organization time to digest one challenge before launching another, and to establish clear milestones and review mechanisms to track progress.

At the Core

Next came "The Core Competence of the Corporation" in the May–June 1990 issue of the *Harvard Business Review*. In speaking of the difference in performance between two large corporations NEC and GTE, with NEC outperforming GTE, Hamel and Prahalad noted: "The distinction we observed in the way NEC and GTE conceived of themselves—a portfolio of competencies versus a portfolio of businesses—was repeated across many industries."

In the long run, they asserted, competitiveness derives from "an ability to build, at lower cost and more speedily than competitors, the core competencies that spawn unanticipated products. The real sources of advantage are to be found in management's ability to consolidate corporate wide technologies and production skills into competencies that empower individual businesses to adapt quickly to changing opportunities."

Competencies had come up in the management literature previously, both obliquely and specifically. For example, Ted Levitt in "Marketing Myopia," his famous 1960 *Harvard Business Review* article, emphasized the importance of companies clearly identifying what business they were in. Railway companies are in the business of transportation, for example, rather than that of railways.

The strategy pioneer Kenneth Andrews was more specific in *Business Policy: Text and Cases* in 1965 when he observed that "the 'distinctive competence' of an organization is more than what it can do; it is what it can do particularly well." Elsewhere in the same book, he stated, "In each company the way in which distinctive competence, organizational resources, and organizational values are combined is unique." However, Prahalad and Hamel elevated the idea to a different level with their conception of a competitive struggle for and between core competencies.

Harmonic Strategy

So what were core competencies according to Prahalad and Hamel? They were about harmonizing streams of technology, the organization of work, and the delivery of value. They were "communication, involvement, and a deep commitment to working across organizational boundaries" and involved people at many levels in all functions. Indeed, blending skills across functional boundaries was an essential aspect of core competencies.

Instead of viewing a venture as a collection of business units, they wanted managers to see the organization as a portfolio of core competencies. Corporate strategy was not a static planning exercise or primarily the remit of a finance function with a focus on control and the profit and loss (P&L). Nor did it merely entail the detailed analysis of competitors, an industry, or the external environment. Instead, strategy was active and far more wide-ranging across an organization and required an internal assessment of the resources a firm had at its disposal and what could be done with those resources.

The same year that *Competing for the Future* appeared, a collection of perspectives on "the theme of core competence and the processes and issues involved in managing core competence" was published.[6] In its foreword Richard Rumelt identifies a number of key elements of the core competencies concept as proposed by Hamel and Prahalad:

> **Corporate span.** Core competencies transcend business units and products in a company. Instead they run across the entire organization, and support the potential value of many products or businesses within that organization.

> **Temporal dominance.** While a product is the expression of an organization's core competencies at a particular moment in time, core competencies themselves are more stable, emerging and evolving over time, often many years.

> **Learning by doing.** Competencies are a product of collective learning in an organization and are enhanced as they are applied and shared.

Competitive locus. Organizations are, effectively, a portfolio of core competencies and disciplines. Product competition in the market is merely an expression of competition at a more fundamental competency level, which is itself founded on skills acquisition.

Core competencies are not individual skills or technologies. Rather, they are bundles of capabilities that are made up of bundles of skills, knowledge, insight, and experience. It is this collection of competencies that creates an organization's competitive advantage. The dynamic nature of the competencies allows firms to adapt and respond to the changing business landscape, and focusing on the organization's future capabilities is particularly important in this context.

After the exposure Hamel and Prahalad's ideas received and the association of core competencies with firm differentiation and competitive advantage, organizations around the world set out to determine their core competencies.

Hamel and Prahalad offered three tests to identify core competencies. First, a core competency provides potential access to a wide variety of markets. Second, a core competency should make a significant contribution to the perceived customer benefits of the end product. Third, a core competency must be difficult for competitors to imitate and will be if it is "a complex harmonization of individual technologies and production skills."

Hamel and Prahalad did not expect firms to produce too many core competencies. "Few companies are likely to build world leadership in more than five or six fundamental competencies," they wrote. "A company that compiles a list of 20 to 30 capabilities has probably not produced a list of core competencies."[7]

However, other commentators noted that in practice identifying core competencies was not straightforward. It was not easy to find competencies that met Hamel and Prahalad's tests of providing access to a wide variety of markets, making a significant contribution to the customer benefits of the end products, and being difficult to imitate.

There was always a risk that a session of finding core competencies would result in a wish list of what the company wanted to be good at. There was also the temptation to identify too many core competencies despite Prahalad and Hamel's warning in this respect. Alternatively, some firms approached the search for core competencies from a personal competency standpoint and then tried to work back to corporate core competencies. This was not what Hamel and Prahalad had in mind.

What if, as is possible in an age of knowledge-driven enterprise, the core competencies of a firm are bound up with a select few individuals? If these people leave, the company loses its core competencies.

Another potential complication, some have suggested, is that once a company had determined its core competencies, it then felt obliged to exploit them as much as possible. That frequently meant diversification, a route littered with potential pitfalls.

A New Revolution

Hamel and Prahalad were advancing their ideas on strategy at a time of rapid change. When "The Core Competence of the

Corporation" was published in 1990, the Internet, one of the biggest game changers of the twentieth century, was still in its infancy; Larry Page and Sergey Brin, the founders of Google, had yet to meet, and Microsoft Windows OS was barely five years old and on version 3.0. Yet just a few years later, the world was riding the crest of the dot-com wave.

Hamel and Prahalad's resource-based perspective on strategy bridged the gap between the strategic-positioning, external environment–biased view of strategy, rooted in the static strategic planning tradition, and the far more fluid and fragmented approach to strategic management suggested by future-oriented thinkers in the field.

Both Hamel and Prahalad predicted this shift and continued to work on different aspects of strategy into the 2000s. The signs that they understood the way the world was changing were clear. Take Hamel's work around the time of *Leading the Revolution*, at the end of the twentieth century. With any luck, he suggested, embracing innovation would allow a company to engage in business concept innovation. And the company should also think differently about competencies, not only in terms of its own core competencies but in terms of "How do I look at all the competencies that are out there in the world and think about the possibilities of putting those things together?"

Life After Core Competencies

As their careers progressed, both Hamel and Prahalad turned to other areas of interest. In 1995, Hamel cofounded the global innovation and strategy consulting firm Strategos, and in the 2000s his attention turned to management innovation and the

founding of the Management Innovation Lab with London
Business School's Julian Birkinshaw.

When we talked with Hamel, he was full of revolutionary
zeal and began by talking about what he calls creative strategizing.

What is creative strategizing?

Mostly it will take revolutionary thinking along a
few key lines. First, strategic planning is not strategy.
Planning and strategic formulations are very different
things. Strategy is discovering and inventing, which
makes strategy subversive and the strategist a rule
breaker, or revolutionary.

Second, the real barrier to strategic planning is
generally at the top, not in the middle or at the bottom. The objective of the revolutionary is to free the
process from the tyranny of the past. Its guardians
are at the top. And third, you cannot expect to see
the end at the start. The strategic formulation is a
discovery process and a moment of invention. It is
not selling to those in the middle and at the bottom
something already defined by those at the top or by
outsiders (the external consultants).

Where will this creativity come from?

Successful strategizing is dependent on four conditions in the organization:

1. It is necessary to include new voices in the
   strategic formulation (if you always have the
   same panel, the conversation is repetitive).

2. It is necessary to bring a new perspective.
3. It is necessary to create strategic conversations about the future of the corporation.
4. It is necessary to have passion.

You're talking about a dramatically different perspective on strategizing.

We like to believe we can break strategy down to five forces or seven Ss, but you can't. Strategy is extraordinarily emotional and demanding. It is not a ritual or a once-a-year exercise, though that is what it has become. We have set the bar too low. As a result, managers are bogged down in the nitty-gritty of the present, spending less than 3 percent of their time looking to the future.

Later, when we next spoke to Hamel, his agenda was that of employee engagement. We asked what he regarded as his core competency:

If I've had any impact on management, and that's for others to judge, I think it might be for the following set of reasons. Number one, I'm very interested in the world of practice. Theory is fine, but only if it helps us do something practical in a new and better way. And so I think I have a love for making a real difference, for trying things out, for mucking in.

Number two, none of these problems for me are intellectual problems. They're not even really about how to make organizations more effective. I'm motivated by human problems. The challenge today is that our organizations need to become more adaptable, more innovative, more engaging. Interestingly, human beings are already all of these things. I know many people who've changed careers in midlife, which takes a huge amount of personal resilience, and people who've dealt with some family tragedy.

As we've democratized the tools of innovation, we're learning that there's this deep seam of creativity in people, and human beings are pretty engaging—we are interested in other people. That's why we watch reality television and so on. So you start to ask yourself, Why is it that our organizations are less human than the people who work there? And why is it that we can't bring all of that humanity to work? And so I think for the first time probably in 100 years and more, the only way you can build an organization that's fit for the future is by building one that's truly fit for human beings. That gives you licence to do a lot of things and try a lot of things that they're simply not going to give you if they think you merely have an intellectual interest or if you have primarily a selfish interest.

And then I think the last piece is: you have to be a contrarian. I don't know where that spirit comes from, but I think you have to think like an outsider; you have to be constantly challenging the conventional wisdom. You can't take anything for granted, and the moment you say to yourself, I've figured this out, I know how it works, you're captured. When I talk to CEOs, often, if I'm learning about a new business, a new industry, a CEO will often say to me, "Gary, let me tell you how our industry works." And I always think, For now, or as far as you know, or until it doesn't. And so I think in the world we live in today, one of the most important personal disciplines for anybody is to regard everything you believe as merely a hypothesis and to be forever uncertain about those beliefs and forever willing to challenge them. So I think it's that combination of hopefully being empathetic and being a bit of a contrarian, constantly circling from the world of theory into the world of practice and back. Those are some of the personal things that have helped me, at least in my own career.

Bottom Up

Meanwhile, Prahalad focused on the co-creation of value and the innovation challenges at the bottom of the pyramid, together with his academic colleague Venkat Ramaswamy, coauthoring *The Future of Competition: Co-Creating Value with Customers* and following up with *The Fortune at the Bottom of the Pyramid: Eradicating Poverty Through Profit* and his final book, *The New Age of Innovation* (2008), coauthored with M. S. Krishnan, before his untimely death in 2010, at a time when he was considered the leading management thinker in the world.[8]

We were fortunate to get to know C.K. over the years and always found him engaging and generous company. As we wrote in a Thinkers50 tribute to him, C.K. was unique among the management theorists we have met. He combined the intellectual detachment of a business school professor with the humanity of a social activist.

An enduring memory of C.K. is something that happened after the filming of a Thinkers50 interview with him. The interview had gone well. The interviewee (C.K.) had given a brilliant performance. However, the interviewer (Des) had stumbled over some of the questions. Despite the fact that he was tired after a long day and had a plane to catch, C.K. uncomplainingly did several retakes. Finally, the interview was in the can and he was free to go. Most gurus would have left with barely a backward glance. But C.K. turned to the camera crew and asked: "Did I make sense to you? Because if I didn't, then I'm not doing my job properly."

The camera crew had been drafted at short notice. An hour earlier they had probably never heard of him. Certainly they had never read any of his books or articles. Yet the response was emphatic. They had understood. More than that, they instinctively recognized that here was not just a clever man but also a great man. It was the only time we can remember a camera crew spontaneously asking for the autograph of a business school professor.

That was C.K. "The hidden thread that runs through my work is the idea of the democratization of commerce," he told us when we last spoke. "That is what I care about." He cared passionately that his ideas were understood not just by academics and MBAs but by everyone. C.K.'s reasoning was compellingly simple: his ideas were *for* everyone.

His mission was to bring a more humane and generous view of capitalism to the attention of the world. Think of it as a more sustainable strategy not just for capitalism but for humankind.

When we last talked, shortly before he died, it was this theme, which was at the heart of his final book, *The New Age of Innovation*, that he expounded on.

What is the golden thread that links all of your work?
The hidden thread—which is no longer hidden because I have told you about it—is the democratization of commerce. That is what my books have been building up to.

If you think about the democratization of commerce, I started with a broad philosophical perspective. The twentieth century was about political freedom. I'm not Pollyannaish. I recognize it is a work in process. We are not there yet. But people recognize that political freedom is a birthright. So now I ask myself, What is the big challenge for all of us in the twenty-first century? It's how to democratize commerce.

Think about core competences as an idea. Core competence is not about top management; it's about ordinary workers, ordinary people, the ordinary technical community, and the worker community working together to create intellectual capital. We are basically saying that intellectual capital is critical for companies to succeed, so don't underestimate the value added and the criticality of ordinary people. It's not all the top guys.

Now the idea's widely accepted. And thanks to TQM [Total Quality Management], which is exactly that, everybody understands that quality is about ordinary people being empowered. That's the starting point. Then you move to the second idea of co-creation. Co-creation is an important idea. What it says is that we need two joint problem solvers, not one. In the traditional industrial system, the firm was the center of the universe, but when you move to the new information age, consumers have the opportunity to shape their own personal experiences.

So with co-creation, consumers can personalize their offerings and the firm can benefit. Co-creation is about saying, How do we empower consumers? So I started with empowering employees inside; that is the core competence idea. Co-creation is the next part: How do you empower both suppliers and consumers so collectively we can create bigger value?

These days, connecting with suppliers is called connect and develop or open innovation. This idea has not suddenly happened; it's an old idea. But co-creation with consumers is happening all over the place, and *The New Age of Innovation* is all about how to make it happen.

What's an example of that kind of co-creation?

Think of Google. Google does not tell me how to use the system; I can personalize my own page; I can create iGoogle. I decide what I want. Google understands that it can have a hundred million consumers, but each one can do what they want with its platform. That is an extreme case of personalized co-created value. We call that N = 1.

On the other hand, Google does not produce the content at all. The content comes from a large number of institutions and individuals around the world. Google aggregates it and makes it available to me. So resources are not contained within the firm but accessed from a wide variety of institutions; therefore, resources are global. Our shorthand for that is R = G.

And that ties in with the democratization of commerce?

Yes. So I started with a firm-centric view, the democratization process breaking the hierarchy and allowing ordinary people to contribute. That's about as anti–scientific management as you can get. Taylor said to workers, "I will make you more efficient by breaking down your work into simple actions so that you don't have to think." With the core competencies idea, we were saying to workers, "We want you to think." Now I am saying, "I want suppliers and consumers to think with me." And that is the co-creation idea.

Then if you put the two together and you go down to the bottom of the pyramid, you're essentially saying, How do I get all people in the world to have the benefits of globalization as consumers, producers, innovators, and investors? So think of the world as a combination of microconsumers. That means you have to make things affordable. That is the bottom of the pyramid, accessible and available.

As microconsumers I also want them to exercise choice. That's co-creation. And that applies across the board. Even if you can afford what rich people can afford, you still want to co-create. In other words, personal choice and affordability are two sides of being the consumer. As a microproducer, I also want to get paid fairly for my work. That means I have to become part of a supply chain globally. Whether I'm a poor Kenyan farmer exporting flowers to Europe or an Indian drug maker exporting the products to the United States, I want to be paid fairly. That means we have to connect all people to markets, not only the local markets but global and regional markets.

Two other aspects are equally important in co-creation. Everyone can be a microinnovator because the connectivity today allows people everywhere to participate and be useful. So what we see today is a larger number of people participating in solving problems. It allows you or me to be a microinnovator. And finally, the next big step is to say, How do I get people to invest small amounts, $3, $4, $5, whatever they can afford? How do we aggregate them so that everybody participates in increasing the productivity of capital?

So the idea of democratization is building systems based on the individual, where a microconsumer can be a microproducer, microinnovator, and microinvestor? Intellectually I've been deeply concerned about the criticality of the individual. So the democratization of commerce forces us to think about three issues in a very important way. First is the centrality of the individual, not institution-centrality of the individual but the individuals of the institution. So that's the centrality of the individual. Interdependence of institutions; nobody can do this alone any longer. It doesn't matter how big the company is. That's why even companies like Procter & Gamble have to think about connect and develop. Everybody now understands that. That means you have to compete as an equal system: interdependence of institutions.

And the third part, which is more important, is about interactive innovations, which involve a large number of people. And that is why in *The New Age of Innovation* I try to coin simple terms.

You use the formulas N = 1 and R = G. Can you explain what they mean in the context of democratizing commerce?

N is equal to one—that is the centrality of the individual experience. R is equal to G, which by definition is the interdependence of institutions. And finally, I am arguing for interactive, iterative innovation rather than just hoping for the big, radical breakthrough, which may happen. A lot of things in life can be achieved with small steps taken very rapidly by a large number of people, creating big change.

And you can see what has happened with Facebook and Twitter and LinkedIn. There are fundamental changes in our society taking place so rapidly, seamlessly, and painlessly. In other words, nobody's forcing you to be part of it, but you see the benefits, you are part of it; if you don't see it, you're not.

And so I think we are on the verge of this new intellectual challenge, and certainly an organizational and social challenge, of how do we allow everybody to participate in the benefits? That does not mean everybody gets to be equally successful, but everybody has the right to participate and the opportunity to participate. At least that is my hope for where we are going.

Beyond the Core

The debate about core competencies ignited by Hamel and Prahalad revolves around the ability of companies (and individuals) to identify what they are good at and then focus on and maximize those competencies.

Among those exploring this territory from another perspective is Bain & Company's Chris Zook. The head of Bain's worldwide strategy practice, he is the author of *Profit from the Core* and *Repeatability*, among other works. When we spoke to Zook, he identified two central themes to his research.

Tell us something about your writings.
First, all of my books are about how companies seek—successfully or not—their next wave of profitable growth. Where do companies go next? What is the balance between focus and going into new areas?

And number two, maybe even more interesting than that, is the consistent revelation through all the research and all the case studies that more often the main barrier to companies finding their next wave of growth is themselves, that the answer is internal. Only 15 percent of the variation in performance among companies is related to choice of market, and 85 percent is related to how those businesses compete against others around them. And when we actually look at the main issues and barriers that companies have in that regard, we find more of them tend to be internal than external. Businesses can tend to be their own enemies, and self-awareness at the end of the day is probably at the epicenter of a lot of the great success stories and great failure stories in business.

Should we find that depressing or uplifting?

I think in a funny way it's actually uplifting, because ultimately, it's very empowering, and a lot of the great iconic stories that we've used through the 12 years of research on this topic have been about companies that somehow lost their way or stalled out. Maybe companies like LEGO, which went into theme parks and children's watches and began to think of themselves as a brands company, went back to the core LEGO toy, exited everything else, and were completely rejuvenated. American Express is a similar story. In the Netherlands, Vopak a number of years ago was a similar story. And even for many large corporations, like Procter & Gamble, it stalled out and realized it had gone into cosmetics and pharmaceuticals and perhaps underinvested in its original core of brand management and deep ability to commercialize consumer insight faster than many of its competitors.

It's actually very empowering that more often than not the answer lies within. We looked at 115 major studies we did for companies around the world and asked what was the essence of the core insight, the seminal insight, from looking at all the possible strategic options for the business. And in two-thirds of the cases, we found that the seminal insight was that the business had radically underestimated the full potential of its deepest strengths and that actually the answer was more readily apparent and more possible than moving to a new market, which is an extraordinarily risky and dangerous proposition.

How can we wean companies from diversification?
The key is, number one, to have a CEO who is not ego-driven, wanting to build empires and pursue bright, shiny objects, but a CEO ideally who loves the core of the business. Often we find that a reinjection of the founder's mentality causes the business to return to its roots and very often to rediscover things that were there; think of the return of A. G. Lafley at Procter & Gamble or Howard Schultz at Starbucks.

So I think it really is the mentality of the management team and an intellectual curiosity and a love of the essence of the core business itself at the front line which keeps businesses out of trouble. Whereas

I think the business management teams that are obsessed with the pursuit of hot markets and growth goals set in a vacuum are the businesses that tend to get into the most difficulty. Lack of self-awareness combined with ego combined with excessive funds combined with excessive growth goals is probably the worst combination you can have. You need to look after them, but you also need to understand what they are.

What is your core? is one of the hardest questions for businesses to consistently answer. You can do many great things in business, but if you're doing them identically to all the competitors around you, prices will be bid down and you won't gain an unusual amount of market share; you'll split it evenly. And so the businesses that do the best are those that are highly differentiated against their competitors on the most important customer criteria, but this is often very difficult to know. And we found when we studied in great detail 200 companies for the book *Repeatability,* we looked at 900 different ways those companies differentiated themselves, and we sorted them into 15 different groupings and clusters, and we're now trying to build much more of a science around the issue of differentiation.

But if there was one constant through these 15 types, it was that actually the very best businesses have maybe three or four really deep capabilities, really extraordinary strengths.

So for Scania, it would be the science of modularization that allows it to have 40 percent fewer parts than many of its truck competitors. We found that the very best businesses had created a repeatable model with many, many activities, but they were built around two or three or four really strong core areas of strength, and that any of those tended be measurable, observably clear to the organization that they were better at that.

For IKEA it would be designing to a price point, flat-packing so that people could carry it away, and the unique format of the store design. What we found was that the most differentiated businesses had a business model, three deep capabilities that could be measured, and a repeatable model that could be taken and constantly adapted to new segments, new applications, or new geographies. That was really the essence of the power of differentiation. But it's a moving target, and you have to keep investing in it and you have to keep staying ahead through constant improvement and through innovation.

CHAPTER
4

Hypercompetition and Beyond

Michael Porter's strategic positioning and Gary Hamel and C. K. Prahalad's resource-based approaches offer divergent perspectives on the world of strategy. Yet despite their dissimilarities they share a fundamental assumption that remained largely unchallenged into the 1990s: the ultimate objective of strategic management is to obtain sustainable competitive advantage and therefore that sustainable competitive advantage is not just desirable but also possible.

But by the mid-1990s, doubts were setting in. Was competitive advantage inevitably ephemeral? Was sustainable competitive advantage a fiction of the strategist's imagination, and creating it the management equivalent of alchemy? Richard D'Aveni of Tuck

Business School certainly thought so. He argued that business was entering a new era of what he called hypercompetition. As competition accelerated and intensified, said D'Aveni, there was no such thing as sustainable competitive advantage. Instead, firms must compete on the basis of fleeting and constantly changing competitive advantages, seeking to destabilize their rivals.

With relish, D'Aveni set himself against the strategy orthodox of the time. This is a position he enjoys. D'Aveni has been called "the Henry Kissinger of corporate strategy." This he takes as a compliment: "I think it's great. I loved Henry Kissinger, and I spent a lot of time reading his books."

At the time, great U.S. corporations such as IBM and General Motors were suffering. Yet conventional strategy theory suggested that those firms, with their huge economies of scale, massive resources, significant pricing power, well-honed supply chains, and cutting-edge R&D, should easily have been able to construct barriers to entry in their markets and secure long-term competitive advantage. Sound familiar?

The world had changed. Long-held tenets of strategy were no longer valid. In this new world, the pace of change accelerates, new technologies are introduced with startling regularity, global competitors emerge, well-established markets vanish, and new markets appear from nowhere.

Instead of the well-established notion that a firm's strategic approach should be to focus on creating advantage, D'Aveni suggested that the destruction of an opponent's advantage is just as important. Firms setting out on a five-year strategy found that by the time the assets were in place and the strategy was under way, market circumstances had altered; the world had moved on, leaving them behind.

In D'Aveni's worldview, corporate survival was bound up with a series of "dynamic strategic interactions." Firms made their strategic moves only to have them countered by competitors, after which a firm sought a different advantage, and was countered once more, and so on. This was the world of hypercompetition, an environment where advantages are rapidly created and eroded.

As D'Aveni wrote in *Hypercompetition: Managing the Dynamics of Strategic Maneuvering*: "Advantages last only until competitors have duplicated or outmaneuvered them . . . protecting advantages has become increasingly difficult. Once the advantage is copied or overcome, it is no longer an advantage. It is now a cost of doing business. Ultimately the innovator will only be able to exploit its advantage for a limited period of time before its competitors launch a counterattack. With the launch of this counterattack, the original advantage begins to erode, and a new initiative is needed."[1]

The strategic goal of organizations in the hypercompetitive world, says D'Aveni, is to "seize the initiative through creating a series of temporary advantages."[2] Organizations stay ahead of competitors by a perpetually leapfrogging from one temporary advantage to the next, creating new advantages and eroding the advantages held by competitors as they go.

In the hypercompetitive environment, dynamic strategic interactions play out across four competitive battlefields: cost and quality, timing and know-how competition, the creation and destruction of strongholds, and the accumulation and neutralization of deep pockets.

D'Aveni also offers a set of principles with which to navigate the hypercompetitive world. To do this he reinvents a well-known framework developed by the management consultants McKinsey. The original 7-S framework specified a number of internal factors that had to fit together to contribute to competitive advantage: structure, strategy, systems, style, skills, staff, and superordinate goals. But, argues D'Aveni, the idea of fit is about maintaining a particular state rather than the evolution of a series of advantages. This is an inflexible approach unsuitable for hypercompetition.

Instead, he offers his own take on the 7-S framework. D'Aveni believes that three things are necessary for firms to disrupt the market: a vision of how to shake up and disrupt markets, certain competencies required to break up the status quo, and the right tactics to deploy in hypercompetitive situations and amid disruptions.

To succeed in these areas, firms should use the seven factors of D'Aveni's new 7-S framework. Those are as follows: First, there is stakeholder focus, and second, strategic soothsaying (vision), focusing on key stakeholders such as customers and employees and predicting what customers will want in the future. Third and fourth are speed and surprise (competencies), moving quickly to take advantage of opportunities and crush counterattacks from competitors without those competitors expecting it. As D'Aveni points out, IBM was seemingly invincible, but Dell blindsided it with its direct sales and distribution model, catching Big Blue unaware.

Then there are three factors relating to tactics. The fifth factor is shifting the rules, where a firm does something that changes the dynamic of a market and the way it operates. Sixth, signals are where a company uses its announcements of strategic intent to dominate its market. Seventh, simultaneous or sequential thrusts are a multiple attack designed to bamboozle and befuddle competitors through a series of developments such as product launches.

Hyperconversation

Face-to-face, D'Aveni has the appealing air of a Damon Runyan character: a big man with incisively large opinions, keen to tackle the big ideas.

> *Tell us about the genesis of* Hypercompetition.
> The book came about because of a very strange event. I went to Cape Cod in Massachusetts for a vacation, and a hurricane came along called Hurricane Bob. While I was there it knocked out all the electricity for about four days. When the electricity came back on, CNN was running a program on the fall of the Soviet Union. I had no idea that something like that could happen in a few days. It was one of the most important economic and political changes of our generation.
>
> So I stepped back and said to myself, I'm teaching all of these students about long-term plans and consistent strategies. How do you really do that in a world where significant earth-shattering changes appear overnight? How do you do that when even if you had all the resources of the Central Intelligence Agency, you still couldn't figure out that it was going to happen? I thought to myself, I must be a fraud,

and decided to sit down and write a book that was about unsustainable advantages in an unpredictable world rather than the traditional view of strategy.

So you described the world we're now in?
Yes, that's right. Except I think the world has become even crazier since 1994; it's really hypercompetition on steroids today. It's even more relevant today than it was when I first bought it. The core idea was that advantages were becoming unsustainable because of globalization and technological disruption. Globalization is accelerating because of the rise of China and India and the falling entry barriers around numerous other countries. Of course, technology hasn't slowed down at all; it's expanding. The Internet, which was once considered revolutionary, is now par for the course everywhere, still having the same radicalization effect on many, many markets. Just we don't talk about it anymore, because it's so endemic in every marketplace.

In such a disorderly, chaotic world, isn't strategy wishful thinking to think we can plan the future in any detail?
Yes, that's the whole point of hypercompetition. What I argued was that there was a need for long-term strategies, strategies about sequencing, lots of short-term advantages and exploring your way forward, the way Lewis and Clark found the Northwest Passage to the Pacific. You only know what direction

you're headed in when you go from hilltop to hilltop looking around for the next hilltop. You can't chart the course all the way from beginning to end the way you might have been able to 20 years ago when things were stable. You can't know where you're going to end up in this kind of world, and you have to be used to the uncertainty. You have to have tolerance for that kind of a world but have the faith and the courage to be able to move forward from hilltop to hilltop and not get caught in the intellectual trap of thinking that you have to continue to leverage the same confidence that you had one year ago or five years ago, because it won't get you to where you're going.

Spheres and Revolutions

A keen reader of military strategists and Sun Tzu, D'Aveni went on to look at spheres of influence and counterrevolutionary measures. Those countermeasures translated into five strategic responses that were correlated with different revolutionary stages. Detect a revolution early enough and companies can use a *containment* approach, says D'Aveni. Throw up some obstacles and hope to quash the revolution before it gains momentum or at least buy some time to deploy the second strategy. This next step involves trying to *shape* the revolution in a way that allows the new technologies or business models to complement rather than replace the incumbent's technologies. If this fails, the company has some time to see if it can modify and *absorb* the new technologies.

Some revolutions gather pace too quickly to quell, shape, or absorb, however, notes D'Aveni. In that case companies need to get more aggressive. One option is to try to *neutralize* challengers head-on by giving away competing benefits for free temporarily, for example. Or the market leader could try to bypass the revolution, using *annulment* strategies.

For his spheres of influence concept, D'Aveni drew on a geopolitical concept usually applied to nations. Spheres of influence are partly the answer to a fundamentally important challenge companies face. As D'Aveni put it: "For a company's portfolio of businesses and geographic market positions, what overall logic can be used to stake out and defend a favorable position within its industry or industries?"[3]

Spheres of influence are "the best way for successful businesses to establish and maintain order and create profitable industries."[4] These spheres consist of a number of layers, each with its own strategic intent. At the core is the product, service, or geographic market that forms the basis of the company's power and profits. Having core competencies focused on this area is not enough to create a sphere of influence; in addition, the company must exert dominance and value leadership over its core markets and maintain control by repelling possible usurpers.

The next layer of the sphere out from the core is that of vital interests. These are product, service, and geographic zones critical to the core. Lose in these markets and the knock-on effect will threaten to displace a company from its prime position in its core. Beyond the realms of vital interests lie the buffer zones: markets that are expendable and as such provide protection against incursions from rivals.

The remaining two zones involved in creating the sphere of influence are, first, pivotal zones that have the potential to tip the balance of competitive power in the future; companies can keep a precautionary interest in these markets. Second, there are forward positions. These frontline products or services are close to the core of key rivals. However, when rivals in turn have forward positions near other key rivals, it creates a situation of mutually assured destruction, a Mexican standoff in which none of the companies are prepared to risk approaching the core of their rivals for fear of being similarly attacked.

Once it is well established, D'Aveni says, a sphere of influence is "a powerful arsenal that enables a company to project its power and come to dominate the larger competitive space of its industry. . . . It also enables astute managers to cajole those outside the sphere to settle into their own well-established borders."[5]

The Threat of Commoditization

By the end of the 2000s, D'Aveni had shifted his sights to a relatively new and increasingly common threat that companies faced: the commoditization of their product or service. Whether through cheaper rivals, technology innovation, or product substitutes, commoditization and falling into what D'Aveni called the commodity trap had "the potential to destroy entire markets, disrupt whole industries and drive previously successful firms out of business."

> *You've said that commoditization is the latest manifestation of hypercompetition. Can you explain that?*
> Commoditization is one of the most virulent forms of hypercompetition. Commoditization is the process of a diamond gradually finding its facets worn off by wind, water, and handling until it becomes simply a

rough stone. And it's similar with products. Products that commoditize basically go from being differentiated to having lost their uniqueness. Most people think the solution is to create a continuous differentiation process to recarve new facets onto the stone. The trouble is that everyone can do the exact same thing. Imitation now is so quick that you end up running faster and faster to stay in the same place. Like the Red Queen in *Alice in Wonderland*, you run so fast that you get nowhere at all.

The first commodity trap you describe is deterioration. How does that work, and can you give an example?
It turns out that not all commoditization takes place in the same way. People have one word for it, but it actually has three heads. One of the heads is deterioration. That method of commoditization is typically wrought by a low-end discounter. The low-end discounter provides such low prices that people buy only on price. The other firms then have to deal with the discounter's market power, and so they start to sink into this hole of low prices and low quality, effectively destroying their own advantages. Alternatively, they move out to become stuck in tiny little niches.

Looking at different industries and companies, such as Walmart in retailing and Ryanair or Southwest in the airline industry, there have been basically three responses: take advantage, escape, or undermine that trap. My favorite response is, rather than succumbing to the market power of that low-end discounter, you seek to undermine it. Several different strategies came to light in my research about how to undermine the strategy of a low-end discounter. One was to find a way to make its power obsolete. Another was to apply another of the commodity traps—proliferation—to the low-end discounter to basically take it out of the market by nibbling at it from multiple directions.

So there's deterioration, there's proliferation, and the final head on the monster is escalation?

Yes, that's right. And this is the toughest one to beat, because momentum builds up. Imagine a price-quality map, and you find players moving toward the corner of low price and high quality. It's a game of one-upmanship. Each player raises her quality, lowers her price, and the next one has to match. It starts to become like the Cuban missile crisis, but it's an arms race to the bottom because the first one to the bottom blows himself up. You end up giving away your product for almost nothing.

So the question is, Can you control the momentum toward that? The potential solutions are to reverse the momentum in one direction, to slow or freeze the momentum, or to harness the momentum so that you move faster than everybody else toward the point of commodity. But then, just as you bring everybody to the commodity cliff, you jump and change the dimensions of the map so that you're no longer playing on the same quality scale and the rest of your industry jumps into commodity hell.

*To continue mixing our metaphors, the financial crisis
revealed another element of commoditization, which
is evaporation. Can you tell us more about that?*
Yes, that's a particular problem showing up during
the recession. Demand evaporation is simply that
people stop buying. They buy so much less than they
did before that all companies have to lower their
prices to sell anything at all. There's excess capacity,
and a lot of price competition develops as a result. So
evaporation isn't really a commodity trap in the traditional sense. It's not the market whittling down the
facets of the diamond; it's really a temporary problem of recessionary periods. And here the solution is
to recognize that you're in a tremendous storm and
batten down the hatches. You also learn how to float
with the changes so that you can be very flexible as
things unfold. And then finally you become able to
preposition yourself for landing on your feet when
the storm subsides.

*In these troubled times, is strategy still important?
Does it still make a difference?*
Yes, at least if you do it right. Even more so today,
I think. A lot of it is about prepositioning for the
future, looking at how you can consolidate the industry, so that when you're done, the industry will be
able to function without excess capacity, and finding
methods where you cooperate with the government,
as in financial services. The financial services industry
doesn't quite get it, but the government is going to

take over a lot more control from individual corporations, and this is a great opportunity, not a threat. On
Wall Street they see it as a threat, but if you can put
in regulations, cooperate to put in all kinds of rules
to prevent another credit crunch, you can also create
tremendous barriers to entry and create a world in
which you're one of the last guys standing. The last
man standing strategy plays out in a lot of industries
today.

How does a strategist keep in touch with the real world?

Basically I'm an importer and exporter of ideas. I
suck up the general trends I see all over the globe and
what I see from the CEOs I invite to my classes; over
the last couple of years I've had about 60 Fortune 500
CEOs come to my classes. Then I look for the trends
and import them across industry boundaries and to
new situations.

I go to many companies where they say, We can't
do that; that's not possible. And I'm able to point out,
Well, why is it possible in these other locations or in
these other industries? So I get to break the frame of
what a lot of people are thinking.

CHAPTER 5

Exploring
Blue Oceans

A decade ago, we found ourselves being escorted through Barbizon, the northern French *village des peintres* that was the home of the nineteenth-century artist Jean-François Millet. Our guides were Professors W. Chan Kim and Renée Mauborgne. "This place is a creative hub," said Kim, smiling broadly as another pack of tourists was disgorged from a bus.

Professors Kim and Mauborgne proceeded to map out their plans to bring together managers from diverse global companies to work on cross-industry and cross-company projects to link innovative ideas to large commercial opportunities. On a wet wintry morning in northern France, it seemed unlikely, but such was the enthusiasm of the duo that we quelled our natural skepticism. At the end of the decade, we were present at a cabinet meeting of a government in Asia, and the practical application of Kim and Mauborgne's ideas was top of the agenda.

Kim, born in Korea, and the American Mauborgne first met at the University of Michigan Business School in the 1980s. At that time, Kim was a professor and Mauborgne was studying. The two academics have worked together ever since, first in the United States and then at INSEAD and also in Asia. As Kim says: "We have been on a long journey sharing an intellectual curiosity to understand what it takes to stand apart and create strong profitable growth."

The paper that set them on the path to strategy success was "Value Innovation: The Strategic Logic of High Growth," published in 1997 in *Harvard Business Review*. Kim and Mauborgne posed the question: "Why is it that some companies succeed in achieving sustained high growth in both revenues and profits?"

The answer, they asserted, concerned a company's approach to strategy. Instead of focusing on staying ahead of the competition, successful companies set out to make the competition irrelevant by adopting a strategic logic the authors termed *value innovation*.

Value innovators differed across five main dimensions of strategy:

1. **Industry assumptions.** Value innovators assume that they are able to alter and shape industry conditions.
2. **Strategic focus.** Instead of responding to rivals, letting their rivals set the parameters for competing, and offering something similar but better, value innovators reinvent markets, making great leaps in the value offered.

3. **Customers.** Rather than focus on segmentation and customization to further refine differing customer needs, value innovators concentrate on customer commonalties among the mass of buyers.

4. **Assets and capabilities.** Value innovators are not contained by viewing business opportunities through existing assets and capabilities, frequently taking a clean slate approach to create new value.

5. **Product and service offerings.** Conventional companies operate within a space defined by the products and services that their industry traditionally offers. Value innovators look for customer solutions that they can meet right across the value chain even if that means entering a new business.

In their paper, Kim and Mauborgne also introduced a new tool, the value curve, to map out value innovation as well as another new tool for managers: the pioneer-migrator-settler map, a three-by-two matrix on which firms could plot their current and planned portfolios to see how balanced they were in terms of their growth potential.

Continuing to develop their strategy ideas in *Creating New Market Space*, published in 1999, Kim and Mauborgne described six patterns of firm behavior "in the way companies create new markets and re-create existing ones." Each pattern of behavior involves looking across a different aspect of a company's business. A company that creates new market space looks at substitute industries instead of focusing on rivals within its own industry; strategic groups within industries rather than competitive position within its own strategic group; the chain of buyers, redefining the buyer group of the business; complementary product and service offerings beyond the bounds of its industry; functional or emotional appeal to buyers, challenging the pricing and feelings-based appeal of the firm's offerings; and across time, anticipating how their market might deliverer value in the future.

In their 2002 article "Charting Your Company's Future," Kim and Mauborgne take aim at the strategic planning process. For most companies, they argue, the strategy planning process lacks clarity. In its place, the strategy experts advocate drawing a strategy canvas. The process involves drawing the "as is" situation and identifying where changes are required, doing some field research, using insights to draft a "to be" strategy canvas and then revising that through a feedback process, and focusing on the projects and actions that close the gaps between the two strategy canvases.

"We started off by looking at the companies that succeeded in circumventing the competition," explains Kim. "Then we moved on to how to create new market space—companies need a way to think and act out of the box if they are to circumvent the competition. Our notion of 'fair process' looks at management decision making and what is required to build and execute creative thinking. Most recently we have looked at how to identify a winning business idea and determine which one to bet on. Qualifying an innovative idea for commercial success is a critical strategy component of value innovation."

Can you give us a definition of value innovation?
Mauborgne: Value innovation is creating an unprecedented set of utilities at a lower cost. It is not about

making trade-offs but about simultaneously pursuing both exceptional value and lower costs.

Although you regard yourselves as pure academics, there seems to be a populist slant to your work. You are asking straight, basic business questions rather than posing abstract hypotheses.

Mauborgne: We ask, Who is doing something interesting? We ask, What is it that makes companies exciting, confident, and strong? Innovation is the life of a company, and we have fun by looking inside companies—both leaders and laggards—to understand the way forward.

We have a natural curiosity. So as our research progresses, we create new hypotheses: Why is it that companies stop innovating and growth slows? How can you find the one idea faster? How do you price something that hasn't been sold before?

Your work suggests that companies often lack insight into the basis of their competitiveness. They don't have all that many answers to your questions.

Mauborgne: That's true. Companies are often unclear about which factors they compete on. They rarely think about alternative industries: the broad range of industries that provide similar products or services. Give companies 20 factors they compete on, and they will agree on 10 but dispute the remainder.

That is a large part of the reason organizations are overtired and lacking in creative momentum.

Because companies often lack a clear, compelling strategy that everyone understands and that sets the company apart, projects are often undertaken that pull the organization in different directions. Individually, a case can be made to justify each project, but collectively, because they are not guided by a unified strategy, the actions do not add up to significant gains.

Strategy, in your eyes, needs to be built around value innovation.

Kim: Our point is that value and innovation are, or should be, inseparable. Value innovation places equal emphasis on value and innovation. Value without innovation can include value creation that simply improves the buyers' existing benefits. Innovation without value can be too technology-driven.

Has the mistake been to equate innovation with advances in technology?

Kim: Yes; value innovation is a strategy concept that is distinct from either value creation or technology innovation. There are plenty of examples of companies that developed technology and then failed to capitalize on it. In video recording technology, Ampex [Corporation] led the way technologically in the 1950s. But value innovators such as JVC and Sony brought the technology to the mass market. There are also many examples of true value innovation occurring without new technology. Look at Starbucks coffee shops, the furniture retailer IKEA, the fashion house of Ralph Lauren, or Southwest Airlines. They are in traditional businesses, but each is able to offer new and superior value through innovative ideas and knowledge.

The power of value innovation lies in engaging people to build collective wisdom in a constructive manner. Value innovation means that the range of disagreement becomes smaller until creativity explodes. Value innovation is fundamentally concerned with redefining the established boundaries of a market. If you offer buyers hugely improved value or create an unprecedented set of utilities to give birth to new markets, the competition becomes unimportant. Instead of playing on the same field, you have created a new one.

Mauborgne: Value innovation enables companies to shift the productivity frontier to a new terrain. Value improvements get you only so far. Value innovation is concerned with challenging accepted assumptions about particular markets, changing the way managers frame the strategic possibilities.

Is the driving force behind value innovation the willingness of companies to create new markets?

Mauborgne: Fundamentally. Innovation occurs across industries, across countries, across companies. These are universal forces. It is therefore irrelevant to categorize organizations by their sector or geographic location. Yet if you look at strategy literature, industry boundaries are usually regarded as central; think of SWOT analysis or Porter's five forces framework.

When we came to Europe, we found companies that were making the move from being supply-driven—outcompeting—to being demand-driven, to actually creating markets, creating new business space. In the United States, there were companies like Home Depot that were vaunted for being different and that were creating new wealth. When we came to Europe, we discovered a rich new vein of examples, companies that were breaking the mold: companies like the Formule 1 hotel chain or Bert Claeys in Belgium. Formule 1 looked anew at the French low-budget hotel market and created hotels attractive to both truck drivers and businesspeople. The Bert Claeys Group built new market space around Belgium's cinemas by refusing to accept common perceptions about what was a declining industry. Bert Claeys ignored long-term decline and created the world's first "megaplex" movie theater with 25 screens and seating for 7,600.

When we talked to these companies, their managers said much the same things as their American counterparts. There was a pattern to their strategies. The big issue for them was not necessarily innovating in terms of technology or science but bringing innovation to bear on the value they delivered to buyers.

Can you explain that further?

Kim: Companies have tended to concentrate on differences between different groups of customers.

They have divided them into ever smaller and neater segments so they can customize their offerings to meet the needs of those segments. We found that value innovators take a different approach. Instead of looking at differences between customers, they focus on the basic commonalities across customers. When companies create unprecedented value on those commonalities, the core of the market is pulled toward them as customers are willing to forgo their individual preferences. Value innovation desegments and collapses established market boundaries by challenging accepted and assumed market order. Unlike the strategy framework built on environmental determinism driven by competition, value innovation takes a constructionist view of the market in which the focus is on shaping the market by cognitive reorderings in managers' strategic thinking.

How can companies use value innovation to create new market space?

Mauborgne: The challenge is to create new demand, what we call market space. New market space is about creating a company's future. Companies can continue to mine their wealth from an existing market space; that's maintenance. They can concentrate on market share. But there is something more: the act of creation. Creating new market space will become increasingly vital.

Creating new market space provides growth. There are two paths to growth. One is the mergers and acquisitions path, which often leads to growth but rarely leads to profitable growth. The other is organic growth by creating new businesses. Although this path is profitable and necessary, in markets where supply exceeds demand, companies are often hesitant because they don't have a path forward to believe that they could succeed in changing things. They need a bridge to get there. Hopefully, some of the ideas and analytics we have been developing will help companies in building that bridge.

What else is needed for companies to grow?

Kim: Another element is our concept of fair process. This has to do with people. Transformation requires that companies earn the intellectual and emotional commitment of their employees. To do so requires a degree of fairness in making and executing decisions. All a company's plans will come to nothing if they are not supported by the employees.

If you violate fair process, it can be devastating. British Airways lost significant ground in employee morale and customer service after it announced a cost-cutting program at a time when its profits were high and its planes were full. It violated fair process in making the plans. There was no engagement, explanation, or clarifying of expectations.

Fair process is based on the simple human need for intellectual and emotional recognition. Without fair process it can be difficult for companies to achieve something their people generally support.

YOU MAY ALSO LIKE...

other retailers or sellers are returnable only to the retailer or seller from which they are purchased, pursuant to such retailer's or seller's return policy. Magazines, newspapers, eBooks, digital downloads, and used books are not returnable or exchangeable. Defective NOOKs may be exchanged at the store in accordance with the applicable warranty.

Returns or exchanges will not be permitted (i) after 14 days or without receipt or (ii) for product not carried by Barnes & Noble or Barnes & Noble.com.

Policy on receipt may appear in two sections.

Return Policy

With a sales receipt or Barnes & Noble.com packing slip, a full refund in the original form of payment will be issued from any Barnes & Noble Booksellers store for returns of undamaged NOOKs, new and unread books, and unopened and undamaged music CDs, DVDs, and audio books made within 14 days of purchase from a Barnes & Noble Booksellers store or Barnes & Noble.com with the below exceptions:

What are the basic questions companies need to ask
themselves if they are to embrace fair process?
Mauborgne: First, they need to ask whether they
engage people in decisions that affect them. Do
they ask for input and allow people to refute the
merit of one another's ideas? Do they explain why
decisions are made and why some opinions have
been overridden? And after a decision is made, is
it clearly stated so that people understand the new
standards, the targets, responsibilities, and penal-
ties? The big U.S. automakers have a history of vio-
lating fair process and have paid the price in results
many times over.

You have moved into the world of predictions with
your work on how to spot winning business ideas.
Surely this is more of an art than a science.
Mauborgne: We have created three analytical tools to
help managers identify a winning business idea whatever market space a company occupies or creates.

　　The first is the Buyer Utility Map, which indicates the likelihood that customers will be attracted
to a new idea. This is a matrix based on six stages
of buyer experience, from how easy it is to find a
product to how easy it is to eventually dispose of it,
and six "customer utility levers," from environmental friendliness to improved customer productivity.
Innovations should occupy as many squares on the
matrix as possible, although it is unlikely to be more
than three or four.

The second tool, the Price Corridor of the Mass, identifies which price will unlock the greatest number of customers. It does this by benchmarking prices not just against similar products but against different products that fulfill the same function. For example, short-haul airlines compete not just against other airlines but against buses, trains, and cars.

The third tool, the Business Model Guide, is a framework for calculating whether and how a company can deliver an innovative product or service at the targeted price. It includes options such as cost targeting and opportunities for outsourcing and partnering.

If you apply the tools, will innovation surely follow?
Mauborgne: Not quite. First, innovation, like all other strategic actions, will always involve both opportunities and risks. Ours are designed to help systematically raise the probabilities of success, shifting the odds in favor of the opportunities over the risks. Innovations also often have to overcome adoption hurdles. There may be resistance from stakeholders both inside and outside the company. Employees, business partners, and the general public can tackle those problems. The key is open discussion with those stakeholders about the impact and ramifications of the innovation. Look at genetically modified food. What if Monsanto had opened up discussions with the stakeholders? Perhaps, instead of being vilified, it might have ended up as the Intel Inside of food for the future, the provider of the essential technology.

Are you still finding new value innovators doing interesting but largely unknown things?

Mauborgne: Constantly. The periphery exists in less-developed countries and in countries not known for value innovation. Peripheral companies include the Hungarian bus company NABI, which is rapidly dominating the U.S. bus market by changing the value curve of the industry, and Cirque du Soleil, the Canadian circus that has led to a rebirth and redefinition of the circus industry. Cirque du Soleil collapses the two industries of theater and circus and in doing so leapfrogs Ringling Brothers and Barnum & Bailey circuses and opens up the entire adult audience for circus at a price point several multiples more than that of a traditional circus. There is also the French company JCDecaux, which is the leading provider of outdoor advertising space. JCDecaux created an entirely new industry space by converting bus stops and metro stations into very desirable advertising space. Municipalities win by getting outdoor furniture that is stylish and free, and JCDecaux wins by selling the advertising spaces in these desirable prime-location city stops.

But surely emulating such peripheral organizations is very difficult and perhaps ill advised or impossible. P&G is not Cirque du Soleil.

Kim: Businesspeople always say there are questions of culture, the stock market, rules and regulations, and so on. Yet whenever we show the Formule 1 example, people say, "Why can't we do that in my industry?" The challenge is not to emulate what any of these companies did but to understand the thinking process that allowed them to create a new market and value innovations. Companies find this challenge inspiring. Learning to think differently about opportunities and risks, daring to move forward into the future—that is what keeps people and companies alive, young, and growing.

You appear quite prepared to commercially share your concepts and the notion of value innovation.
Kim: We gain more by giving people the value innovation trademark free of charge so long as they share their knowledge and research findings. It is an open-system approach. They tell us what works and what doesn't work. The more empirical evidence and market feedback we have either against or for our hypotheses, the richer the concepts we can build for theory and practice.

Moves and Patterns

It was in 2004 that Kim and Mauborgne struck strategy gold with their *Harvard Business Review* article "Blue Ocean Strategy" and the follow-up book of the same name. They began by looking at the basic units of analysis used at that time in the strategy business literature: the company or the industry.

"We found that the pace of industry creation has speeded up," says Mauborgne. "We asked which industries are around that weren't around in 1900. And it turns out that most of the industries we take for granted today did not exist at that time. The same can be said if we look back only 30 years. We have a hugely underestimated capacity to create new industries. Everyone assumes that the number of industries stays the same over time, but it doesn't."

Kim and Mauborgne's analysis of industry history reveals that it is not the company or the industry that is the right unit of analysis for explaining the root of profitable growth. Instead, they found that an industry's and a company's ups and downs are substantially attributable to something they call *strategic moves*. "By strategic move we mean the set of managerial actions and decisions involved in making a major market-creating business offering," they note.

Lasting success in business does not come from battling against competitors because as rivals fight over shrinking profits, cutthroat competition results in a bloody red ocean. Success comes from creating blue oceans: untapped new market spaces with high growth potential.

"The moment you take an industry-deterministic view of your company, you are a victim of that industry. The moment you sit back and ask how can we create a whole new industry, then you start to break that cycle. All industries are created not by big resources but by big ideas," says Kim.

Kim and Mauborgne studied over 150 of these strategic moves—moves that have delivered products and services that opened and captured new market space with a significant leap in demand—from over 30 industries, spanning from 1880 to 2000, to understand the pattern by which blue oceans are created and captured and high performance is achieved.

Blue ocean strategy is about risk minimization and not about risk taking, they say. Of course, there is no such thing as a riskless strategy. Any strategy, whether red or blue, will always involve risk. Nonetheless, when it comes to venturing beyond the red ocean to create and capture blue oceans, there are six key risks companies face: search risk, planning risk, scope risk, business model risk, organizational risk, and management risk. The first four risks revolve around strategy formulation, and the latter two around strategy execution.

Each of the six principles in *Blue Ocean Strategy* expressly addresses how to mitigate each of these risks. The first blue ocean principle—reconstruct market boundaries—addresses the search risk of how to identify, out of the haystack of possibilities that exist, commercially compelling blue ocean opportunities. The second principle—focus on the big picture, not the numbers—tackles how to mitigate the planning risk of investing lots of effort and lots of time but delivering only tactical red ocean moves. The third principle—reach beyond existing demand—addresses the scope risk of aggregating the greatest demand for a new offering.

The fourth principle—get the strategic sequence right—addresses how to build a robust business model to ensure that you make a healthy profit on your blue ocean idea, thereby mitigating business model risk. The fifth principle—overcome key organizational hurdles—tackles how to knock over organizational hurdles in executing a blue ocean strategy addressing organizational risk. The sixth principle—build execution into strategy—tackles how to motivate people to execute blue ocean strategy to the best of their abilities, overcoming management risk.

Once an organization has an idea, once it has developed an innovative blue ocean strategy, the next step is to implement it. Executing the idea is often the greatest challenge. It is a challenge that all organizations face.

Kim and Mauborgne identify four hurdles to overcome during strategy implementation: cognitive—alerting employees to the need for a change in strategy; limited resources—the greater the shift in strategy, the greater the resources required to effect it; motivation—getting key players in the organization to put their weight behind change; and politics.

Following Up

Next Kim and Mauborgne looked at the perennial strategic talking point of strategy and structure. In their 2009 article "How Strategy Shapes Structure," they argued that there are two main types of strategic approaches. One they called the *structuralist* approach. This involves basing strategy on an assessment of the commercial environment. It assumes, say Kim and Mauborgne, that "a firm's performance depends on its conduct, which in turn depends on basic structural factors such as number of suppliers and buyers and barriers to entry. It is a deterministic worldview in which causality flows from external conditions down to corporate decisions that seek to exploit those conditions."

This is not the way strategy development has to work, though, they argue. As blue ocean strategy shows, structure does not need to shape strategy.

"Blue ocean strategy has its roots in the emerging school of economics called endogenous growth, whose central paradigm posits that the ideas and actions of individual players can shape the economic and industrial landscape," write Kim and Mauborgne. "In other words, strategy can shape structure. We call this approach 'reconstructionist.'"

Although the structuralist approach may be the right approach, there are times when the *reconstructionist* approach is more appropriate. The challenge is to choose the right approach.

In assessing the right way forward, one must consider three factors: the structural conditions that the organization operates in, its resources and capabilities, and its strategic mindset. When structural conditions and resources and capabilities do not make it clear which approach to take, it will depend on the organization's strategic mindset. By strategic mindset, Kim and Mauborgne suggest that innovative organizations that are sensitive to the risks of missing future opportunities will do better with a reconstructionist (blue ocean) approach. Firms that tend to adopt defensive positions and are not keen to venture beyond core activities do best with a structuralist approach.

Once they have chosen the right approach for the circumstances, the firm's managers must develop and align one of three strategy propositions: a value proposition to attract buyers, a profit proposition enabling a company to make more money from its value proposition, or a people proposition motivating the people working for or with the company to implement the strategy.

The three strategy propositions correspond to the traditional activity system of an organization. The outputs of an organization's activities are value for the buyer and revenue for itself, and the inputs are the costs to produce them and the people to deliver them. "Hence, we define strategy as the development and alignment of the three propositions to either exploit or reconstruct the industrial and economic environment in which an organization operates," write Kim and Mauborgne.

The reconstructionist and structuralist approaches to strategy diverge in the way they apply these propositions. As Kim and Mauborgne note: "Under a reconstructionist strategy approach, high performance is achieved when all three strategy propositions pursue both differentiation and low cost. This alignment in support of differentiation and low cost enables a company to open new market space by breaking the existing value-cost trade-off."

Failure to align these three fundamental strategy propositions is one of the main reasons innovations that promise to launch in blue oceans, creating new markets, ultimately capsize.

Talking Red and Blue

In conversation, Kim and Mauborgne have intriguingly contrasting personalities. Kim is passionate and vociferous, Mauborgne more considered. But they sing from the same strategic songbook.

> *You are critical of the language used in discussing business strategy. Why is that?*
> **Mauborgne:** The essence of business strategy can be traced to military strategy. That's why traditionally the field of strategy talked about headquarters rather than head office. In terrain and war there's only so much land that exists. Fundamentally, that explains why business strategy, including competitive strategy, has been predominantly based on how you divide up

an existing pie. It's about relative power. It's a zero-sum game because you cannot multiply the amount of land available.

The question is: Why has the field of business strategy sometimes implicitly, sometimes explicitly taken this assumption to be true? Although strategy in war may be limited to dividing up existing non-changeable landmasses, if there is one thing the world has taught us over the last 100 years, it is that in the realm of business the new market spaces that can be created are infinite. What you see if you look historically is that real gains came when people created an entirely new area, a whole new market space. You can create a win-win game. You can create new land. Just think of the number of industries that exist today that did not exist even 30 years ago. Scientifically, we know the amount of chemical compounds that exist has not changed over time. But look at what you had in the beginning: just dinosaurs. And today by creatively combining them in numerous new ways we have Starbucks. What we can buy today in a 7-Eleven store beats what a king like Louis XIV had. The possibilities are endless.

How does such profusion link to your research?
Kim: We looked back at 150 years of data and found that the pace of industry creation has speeded up. We asked which industries were around in 1900 and are still around today, and it turns out that apart from the basic industries such as cars and steel, almost noth-

ing. Look back to the major industries of 1970 and very few, if any, are now significant. The big growth industries in the last 30 years have been the computer industry, software, gas-fired electricity plants, cell phones, and the café bar concept for starters. But in 1970 not one of those industries existed in a meaningful way, and that's just 30 years back. The pattern continues as you dig into the past. The big industries of 1940 aren't those of 1910 and so on. We have a hugely underestimated capacity to create new industries. Everyone assumes that the number of industries stays the same over time, but it doesn't. And if this is where the bulk of wealth has been created, shouldn't the field of strategy systematically explore and understand the path to new market space creation?

The next question we asked was, How come some companies rise and fall? The companies featured in *In Search of Excellence* struggled afterward. Then along comes another bestseller, *Built to Last*, that says the trouble was that a long enough time frame was not considered. Then *Creative Destruction* comes out and says if you take out the industry effects, some of these companies are even underperforming.

Our conclusion is that companies are the wrong unit of analysis. So are industries. Any company is excellent at certain points in time. It depends on the leaders and managers. There's no such thing as a permanently great company or a permanently great industry. But there are permanently great strategic moves. And the strategic move that we found matters centrally is the creation and capturing of new market space.

What do you mean by a strategic move?

Mauborgne: By *strategic move* we mean the actions of players in conceiving, launching, and realizing their business ideas. In each strategic move, there are winners, losers, and mere survivors.

Can you give an example?

Mauborgne: A snapshot of the auto industry from 1900 to 1940 is instructive. Ford's Model T, launched in 1908, triggered the industry's growth and profitability, replacing the horse-drawn carriage with the car for American households. It lifted Ford's market share from 9 percent to 60 percent.

The Model T was the strategic move that ignited the automotive industry. But in 1924, it was overtaken by another move, this time by GM. Contrary to Ford's functional one-color, one-car single-model strategy, GM created the new market space of emotionally styled cars with "a car for every purpose and purse." Not only was the auto industry's growth and profitability again catapulted to new heights, but GM's market share jumped from 20 percent to 50 percent while Ford's fell from 60 percent to 20 percent.

So understanding the context and the right strategic moves is the key to success. There will always be a debate about rising and falling companies and industries. What the Body Shop did was absolutely brilliant. It created a new market space in a highly competitive industry. The problem was that they didn't realize what made it a brilliant strategic move, and when everyone imitated them, they needed to do it again.

Isn't this just industry life cycle?

Kim: There doesn't have to be an industry life cycle. Because people say there is an industry life cycle, we accept it. Look at CEMEX, the world's third largest cement producer, from Mexico. It is challenging the industry life cycle by creating cement as an emotional product, which is also helping to address the country's housing issues. In Mexico, it usually takes about 8 to 10 years to build a house, and you build it room by room. The issue is that whenever people have any cash, they are always spending it on weddings or other ceremonies or on jewelry or other expensive gifts. So CEMEX has turned cement into an emotional product by saying that if you really love somebody, give them cement. Give them a room to build because you are giving them a house, a room; you are giving them a home. They'll have love and laughter. And they have totally rebranded cement as the best gift you can give someone because you are giving them a home. This has taken a flat industry to higher profit margins and turned it into a growth industry. Similarly, the coffee industry was dead until Starbucks came along.

The moment you take an industry-deterministic view of your company, you are a victim of that industry. The moment you sit back and ask, How can we create a whole new industry? you start to break that cycle. All industries are created not by big resources but by big ideas.

CHAPTER 6

Strategy in Action

How is strategy created? Does good strategy really arrive centrally planned, fully formed, in a neatly packaged, ready-to-go form? Or is the process more haphazard, messier? Is it evolutionary? How does strategy actually get made? Such questions remain the subject of lively and perennial debate. Among the most persuasive and authoritative stokers of the debate over the last half century has been the Canadian academic Henry Mintzberg.

A professor of management at McGill University in Montreal, Mintzberg studied mechanical engineering at McGill in 1961 as well as completing a general arts degree in the evenings. He worked in industry in the operational research branch of Canadian Railways between 1961 and 1963. But the lure of academia proved too strong, and he returned to his studies at MIT's Sloan School of Management, where he obtained a PhD in management.

His PhD thesis was titled "The Manager at Work—Determining His Activities, Roles and Programs by Structured Observation" and formed the basis for *The Nature of Managerial Work*, a scientific examination of what managers did or didn't do.

At the same time Mintzberg embarked on a second strand of research challenging the orthodoxies and accepted practice of strategy. His work in the 1970s went back to strategy basics. What exactly is strategy in the organizational context? Where do strategies come from in organizations? Although the topic of organizational strategy was well explored at the time both in academic theory and in practice, there was surprisingly little analysis of the process by which strategies form in organizations. Mintzberg set about rectifying that gap in knowledge.

As Mintzberg notes in his 1985 paper "Strategies, Deliberate and Emergent" (coauthored with James Waters), strategy was traditionally conceived as something that an organization planned to do in the future. As such, strategy was seen as a phased process of analysis and planning followed by implementation. Mintzberg took a different approach. He theorized that strategy was "a pattern in a stream of decisions." He used this definition to research the phenomenon of strategy formation more easily, as it was possible to separate out streams of behavior and identify patterns within those streams. In particular, Mintzberg was able to examine the relationship between what leaders planned for and intended to do and what actually happened.

The Strategy Process

Mintzberg describes 10 different types of strategy process. At the two extremes lie the infrequently encountered pure deliberate and emergent strategies. In between, strategies range from the deliberate to the emergent. Planned strategy originates from a formal planning process involving the central leadership and involves formal controls to help make sure it stays on track. Entrepreneurial strategy originates from a central unarticulated vision that belongs to a single leader, often the founding entrepreneur. Ideological strategy is driven by the collective ideology of those involved in the organization, is controlled through indoctrination and socialization, and is highly deliberate.

Umbrella strategies exist in which there is lighter central control. Instead leaders set guidelines, goals, and boundaries and then allow others to operate within those guidelines and boundaries to achieve their goals. Thus, these strategies are a mixture of deliberate, emergent, and deliberately emergent. Process strategies are also deliberate, emergent, and deliberately emergent as they are very similar to umbrella strategies in terms of the control exercised by the leaders. However, in this case the leaders control the process of strategy while leaving the content to the discretion of others.

When strategy is driven by individuals or groups of individuals independent of the leadership, Mintzberg called it unconnected strategy. In this case the strategy is emergent from the perspective of the organization but potentially deliberate or emergent from the perspective of the individual creating the strategy in question.

Mintzberg cites the example of the output of the National Film Board of Canada from the 1940s to the mid-1960s, during which time among its many movies there was a small stream of experimental films. Almost all of those films were made by one director. From the board's perspective, the experimental film strategy was emergent. From the perspective of the director, however, it may have been deliberate or emergent. We can't know, though, because the director did not state his intentions on this point.

Consensus strategy is clearly emergent. It originates from consensus among individuals within the organization, where the individuals converge on a particular theme without prior intention. It is collective actions rather than the intentions of central management that are at work here. Finally, there are imposed strategies driven by external circumstances and environmental influence. However, even imposed strategies are rarely entirely emergent, as they are often deliberately modified internally, within the organization.

Five Ps

In 1987 Mintzberg offered five definitions of strategy for consideration: plan, ploy, pattern, position, and perspective.[1] Strategy is perhaps most commonly envisaged as a plan, a consciously intended action developed in advance. A related concept is strategy as a ploy: a specific maneuver designed to outfox opponents. Strategy as pattern, the focus of much of Mintzberg's research, is consistency of behavior, intended or otherwise. Strategy can be a position, an organization locating itself in an environment as Mintzberg describes it. This definition of strategy is consistent with the preceding definitions; an organization can position itself via a plan, as a plan, or as a pattern of behavior. Finally, suggests Mintzberg, there is strategy as a perspective. In this instance it is effectively the ingrained perspective the organization has, its collective and shared outlook on the world.

In his McKinsey Award–winning article "Crafting Strategy," Mintzberg consolidates his existing ideas around strategy formulation, using a craft metaphor, specifically that of the potter; Mintzberg's wife was a potter. Craft, said Mintzberg, suggests a situation in which formulation and implementation merge into a fluid process of learning through which creative strategies evolve.

At the same time Mintzberg extended his concept to include a number of factors involved in crafting strategy. Managing strategy is mostly about managing stability rather than instigating change. The skill lies in knowing when to promote change, says Mintzberg. Detecting subtle discontinuities, breaks in the normal patterns, that threaten the future of the business is another skill required to craft strategy. Managers must also have an intimate personal knowledge of their business: costs, supply chain, products, and customers, for example. Armed with that knowledge, managers should be able to detect and manage patterns of activity or behavior as they emerge and take steps to nurture them.

Finally, managers have to balance and reconcile change and continuity. This involves judging when to continue exploiting existing strategies and when to displace old patterns and pursue new ones. Success here involves the manager blending the past, present, and future.

Over the following years Mintzberg explored various facets of strategy, investigating why organizations need strategies, strategy and leadership, and strategy in the financial services industry, education, and public policy. His next major contribution was the 1994 book *The Rise and Fall of Strategic Planning: Reconceiving the Roles for Planning, Plans, Planners.*

Mintzberg notes that *The Rise and Fall of Strategic Planning* is "very critical, though it ends on a positive note." Mintzberg's book is, to begin with at least, fairly pessimistic about the state of strategy in the corporate world. Key to Mintzberg's view is the distinction between strategic planning and strategic thinking. Strategic planning gets in the way of strategic thinking, he asserts. Planning is about analysis and breaking down goals into a series of rational and logical steps. Planning is "a formalized system for codifying, elaborating and operationalizing the strategies which companies already have."

Strategic thinking, by contrast, is about intuition and creativity and results in loosely articulated visions about direction and objectives. Strategic insight does not come on cue; it needs the right conditions to emerge, usually, says Mintzberg, through the messy process of informal learning.

Mintzberg identifies a grand fallacy that prevents organizations from approaching strategy formulation in a productive way. There is an assumption that "because analysis encompasses synthesis, strategic planning is strategy making." This in turn is predicated on three more fallacious assumptions.

The first is that prediction is possible. Forecasting techniques are limited by the fact that they tend to assume that the future will resemble the past. This gives artificial reassurance and leads to the creation of strategies that are liable to disintegrate as they are overtaken by events. The passion for planning was strongest during stable times such as the 1960s. When the world changes, planners are left seeking to re-create a long-forgotten past.

The second fallacy is that strategists can be detached from the subjects of their strategies, from the reality of the organization. The assumption has been that if strategists are removed from the operations, from the tactics of everyday organizational life, they will be able to discern strategy more effectively. To facilitate this distancing, planners have traditionally been obsessed with gathering hard data on their industry, markets, and competitors. The results are limiting, for example, a pronounced tendency "to favor cost leadership strategies (emphasizing operating efficiencies, which are generally measurable) over product leadership strategies (emphasizing innovative design or high quality, which tends to be less measurable)."

In reality, though, strategists need to understand how strategy is actually formulated in their organizations. Hard data aren't enough. They need soft data: networks of contacts; talking with customers, suppliers, and employees; using the stakeholder grapevine. To gain real and useful understanding of an organization's competitive situation, soft data need to be dynamically integrated into the planning process.

"Strategy-making is an immensely complex process involving the most sophisticated, subtle and at times subconscious of human cognitive and social processes," writes Mintzberg. "While hard data may inform the intellect, it is largely soft data that generates wisdom." They may be difficult to "analyze," but they are indispensable for synthesis: the key to strategy making. As Mintzberg puts it: "Real strategists need to get their hands dirty digging for ideas."

The last fallacy Mintzberg identifies is the assumption that strategy making can be formalized. Strategy formulation has been dominated by an emphasis on logic and analysis. However, this highly structured approach creates a narrow range of options. Alternatives that do not fit into the predetermined structure are ignored. Intuition and creativity must play a more important role. "Planning by its very nature," concludes Mintzberg, "defines and preserves categories. Creativity, by its very nature, creates categories or rearranges established ones. This is why strategic planning can neither provide creativity, nor deal with it when it emerges by other means."[2]

On Safari

On his journey around the wilds of strategic management in *Strategy Safari* (coauthored with Joseph Lampel), Mintzberg identifies 10 different schools of strategy formation, updating and redefining his original 1985 take on strategy types.

The first five are *design*—fitting the internal situation of the organization with the external environment; *planning*—formal planning from analysis of situation to strategy execution; *positioning*, as influenced by the ideas of Michael Porter—strategy depends on the positioning of the firm in the market and within its industry; *entrepreneurial*—strategy driven by the leader; and *cognitive*—delving inward into the minds of strategists.

The second five are *learning*—strategy as an emergent process in which as people come to understand a situation and the organization's ability to deal with it, strategy emerges; *power*—strategy from power games inside and outside the organization; *cultural*—the formation of strategy is tied to the social force of culture; *environmental*—strategy dependent on events in the environment and the company's reaction; and *configuration*—part of a transformational process.

The trouble is that in practice, modern thinking about strategy does not fit neatly into one or another of the 10 schools. More commonly, recent approaches to strategy formation cut across a number of the schools, whether it is resource-based thinking, chaos and evolutionary theory, revolutionary strategy, or strategic maneuvering.

Mintzberg continues to argue that we need a better understanding of the way strategy works. Inexorably, strategy continues to evolve, its development driven by a number of conflicting impulses, collaboration, competition and confrontation, creativity, and the fashioning of new concepts, and the reworking of old ideas. As Mintzberg says at the conclusion of his strategy safari: "We need to ask better questions and generate fewer hypotheses—to allow ourselves to be pulled by real-life concerns rather than pushed by reified concepts. We need better practice, not neater theory. So we must concern ourselves with process and content, statics and dynamics, constraint and inspiration, the cognitive and the collective, the planned and the learned, the economic and the political. In other words, we must give more attention to the entire elephant—to strategy formation as a whole. We may never see it fully, but we can certainly see it better."[3]

How Strategy Works

There may be some cultural significance in the fact that the questioning mantle when it comes to strategy now falls to another Canadian. Roger Martin, former dean of the Rotman School of Management at the University of Toronto, is known for his work on integrative thinking as a means of solving complex problems and has argued that organizations should adopt a more design-based approach to thinking. Designers get close to the end user and use abductive reasoning—pragmatic guesswork—to create more value. They balance two kinds of models of value creation—analytical thinking and intuitive thinking—to produce "design thinking."

The most intriguing aspect of Martin's wide-ranging work is his long-term collaboration with the Procter & Gamble CEO A. G. Lafley. Lafley and Martin are the coauthors of *Playing to Win: How Strategy Really Works.*

Can you explain the big idea behind this book?

The big idea is that you can make strategy simple, fun, and effective. I don't think many people would say their strategy process, the job of putting together a strategy for their company, is any one of those three things. A.G. and I have a belief that you can make strategy very simple; it can be enjoyable to do and very effective, and so we wrote a book about what we did together to do that at Procter & Gamble.

Not many executives really have a definition of strategy that's helpful to them. And so they do lots of analysis, put together very thick documents that sit on shelves, quite famously, and it's because they haven't made a few key choices. What we distilled it down to in our practice is five key choices. If you make those choices, you'll have a strategy. If you haven't made those choices, your strategy is probably not worth having.

So how did the collaboration with A. G. Lafley come about?

When he took over as CEO of Procter in June 2000, he phoned me and said, We've got a lot of challenges and things we need to do. I'd known him for about 10 years prior to that, working on various projects at Procter, and he asked me would I work with him as sort of a counselor and advisor on strategy. So we worked together for the entire time he was CEO and chair of Procter and worked on instilling in P&G a discipline about strategy that he had always believed needed to be there. So we worked together, learned together, and thought we should share the results of that collaboration.

We think that the stories that we can tell about Procter are not just a consultant going in from the outside and interviewing some people; we actually did it and did it together, in a real environment. So we think it has an authenticity to it that is maybe unique.

Tell us about the five questions and how they fit together.

The most important thing about the five questions is that they have to be answered together in a way that reinforces one another. So each of the five questions actually isn't all that hard to answer on its own; it's a little bit harder to answer them in a way that fits together. But the first question is: What is your winning aspiration? So what are you trying to accomplish with your strategy? If you don't have that sense of an objective, it is very hard to have a useful strategy.

Now, many companies have highfalutin aspirations, but those are not then linked to the key choices, which we call the heart of strategy. So that's questions two and three: where to play and how to win. So given your aspirations, where do you want to play in whatever space, whatever market space you're looking at, and then, once you've chosen that, how do you want to win where you've chosen to play? Then the fourth question is, What capabilities do I need to have, to build, to maintain, to win in the place I've chosen to play so that I can achieve my aspirations? And then finally, the last of the five questions is, What management systems do I have to have in place so that I have the capabilities built and maintained so that I can win where I've chosen to play and meet my aspirations?

So it's those five questions that a company needs to answer to have a strategy. The good news is there's no reason why you can't describe that in five pages or less, so you don't need a thick deck of slides. Five pages will do it. In fact, you should be able to summarize it on one page. But the key is that the great strategies are ones where those five things fit together and reinforce one another.

Can you give us an example of that?
We talk about the example of Olay and the transformation it went through from Oil of Olay, a slow-growing, low-price product with an aging demo-

graphic. So that's the brand that we looked at, starting as A.G. took over the beauty category in the late
1990s but then continuing through his presidency.
And we looked at that and said, What are our aspirations for the skin care category?

Well, it turns out that in beauty skin care is
the biggest and most profitable category, a $50 bil-
lion business worldwide. Procter really wanted to get
bigger in beauty. It already had shampoos and condi-
tioners and a little fragrance business, but it wanted
to make that very big. So rather than make it a little
sideline where we had this $750 million brand, which
was low-price and not very important, the aspiration
was to make skin care a centerpiece of a beauty strategy by having a leading brand in skin care.

But then we had a look and asked the question,
Where were we currently playing? Well, where we
were playing was with a product targeted at aging
women, and our demographic was aging. We were
in the wrinkle-prevention, wrinkle-cover-up category.
And our product was sold for about $3.99 for one
little bottle of pink fluid. So we said, Well, is there
another place to play that would open up opportunities for us?

We came to the conclusion that there was a
demographic that was younger, women age 35 to 49,
who were observing the first signs of aging and were
interested in something that helped them with signs
of aging, not just wrinkles but drier skin, spots, blem-
ishes, and the like—what we came to call the seven

signs of aging. So we said if we chose our wheres for these very sorts of skin-involved women, who are a younger demographic, we wouldn't be going dead at the heart of the category.

And then we said, Well, how can we win with these women? What we realized is that we had to dramatically raise the quality proposition of the product, to reposition it as a substitute for what they paid really big bucks for in the department store channel. To do that we had to work with our retail partners to create a kind of a section in the store that made it feel more like the department store channel but was in the store that the buyer was in on a regular basis and also didn't have the pressure of the salesperson at the department store trying to sell you more and more and more stuff.

And so we had to build capabilities, everything from better packaging to better active ingredients. We had to build all sorts of relationships with the beauty editors in the magazines to persuade them to take our product seriously, and we ended up launching Olay Total Effects. We also dropped the "Oil of" prefix and made it Olay: Olay Total Effects, at $18.99, which is a stunningly high price point. So we moved from Oil of Olay at $3.99 to Olay Total Effects at $18.99, but it was positioned in a different place. So it was a different where and a very different how to win. Some additional capabilities were built behind that, and it ended up growing at a 10 to 15 percent rate for over a decade and is now by far the biggest skin care brand in the world, and probably, it's hard to tell exactly, but probably one of the most profitable.

So it's a $2.5 billion and growing business now, all because we set an aspiration, picked a different where, figured out exactly how you had to win, and built the capabilities and the management systems around that. And we believe that's doable in any business as long as you're willing to address those questions and really have an aspiration for winning rather than just playing. Before, we were just playing, and now we're winning.

It's not a linear process, is it? It's very much an iterative process, with one part informing the rest, reinforcing the others.

Yes. That's an important point. There are so many companies that I've observed make their strategy process very linear, and one of the expressions of that is starting out with a long and involved and often painful wordsmithing exercise about what's our vision and mission.

The reason that that takes so long often and there are so many fights is that it's really hard to tell what your aspirations should be until you know a little bit more about where to play and how to win. So you might set your aspiration as something that you cannot find a where to play and how to win that meet it. But if you've already locked and loaded on it and had this whole exercise where we've now got the new vision and we've got the new aspiration, it's hard to then say, Oh oh, we've got to go back. So what we say when we're doing strategy is, set an initial aspiration, then see about a where to play, how to win. If you can't find a where to play, how to win that's consistent with that, maybe go back and revisit it. You can try to create an initial where to play, how to win and then ask, Can we really build the capabilities to win in that way? Oh, maybe not quite. Okay, so we're going to have to tweak it a little bit.

So you're right. It's this iterative process where the key is to frame it that way, to not have everybody say, Oh, no, this is terrible; we've now got to go back and revisit. That's a good part of strategy. That's a great part of strategy. It's what makes strategy powerful.

Are we talking about prototyping strategy?
A.G. and I are both really interested in the world of design, and it borrows some from that. You prototype your strategy decision, and then you look back and say, based on what's happened when we've exposed the prototype to people, Oh, you know, that's sort of right but not quite. And you have that attitude toward strategy, so it doesn't feel like failure, it feels like getting it better and better and better.

Another of the messages of the book is that strategy isn't just for people who are up in the boardroom, that everybody should be doing strategy—whether you're a brand manager or in charge of a business unit, you

should be doing your own strategy—but also that
strategy needs to be done in the context of what the
company's trying to do, in the context of the corporate
strategy. That's the nesting concept you describe. All
the substrategies should fit together seamlessly.

Absolutely. The strategies should fit with each other at
every level in a corporation. So at Procter & Gamble
they have to make strategy decisions about where
to play, how to win at an aspiration at the corporate
level, at the beauty care level, at the skin care level, at
the individual brand level. I encourage the people I
work with, whatever level they're at, to ask the question, What is your aspiration for the part of this company that you are in charge of? Even if it's just one
little department, what's the aspiration? What is your
where to play, how to win choice?

I would even go so far as to say every single person in an organization would be wise to have a where
to play, how to win as an employee. Job descriptions
aren't as specific as put your left foot in front of your
right foot. They sort of say, Well, here's your job. And
within that you have a lot of choices: Where exactly
am I going to focus my time? How am I going to do
that in a way that creates all sorts of value?

Really, the only thing you have to think about in
this nesting concept is that your where to play, how to
win had better reinforce and make more powerful the
where to play, how to win choices of the unit above
you, and the unit above that, and the unit above that.
It's a concept that goes against the CEO making all

the strategy choices because he's way above you, high up in the organization, and you're down below, running a business, and you just execute it.

No. In our view, wherever you are in the organization, you have to make strategy choices too. If everybody felt that they have to make strategy choices, I think corporations would work a lot better than saying we make the choices up above, and you people down there execute. It's not the way the world actually works, and it's not a helpful kind of conception of the corporation.

Where are we in the overall strategy debate? What's changed since Michael Porter's five forces?
One thing that's now a core theme is getting strategy to be effective. So it's one thing for academics to admonish companies to do strategy my way, or some way, or whatever, and then companies not doing strategy and not finding strategy particularly helpful.

So there's one huge theme of making sure strategy is doable by companies, that they can address strategy questions and come to answers.

Then there are these theoretical kinds of debates. A big one has to do with competitive advantage. I think a lot of the debate is not all that helpful. It is obvious that competitive advantage exists in the world. It is also obvious that competitive advantage doesn't last forever. Nothing lasts forever. And if you're trying to say that there is no such thing as competitive advantage, think of all the high-performing, normally profitable companies that have maintained that for years and years and years. It's hard to say that's not competitive advantage.

So the question to me becomes, Is there a thinking process that can help managers make decisions that produce advantage, to create high amounts of value for customers, that enables you to make an attractive return and opens up other possibilities to keep on renewing that? That's the fundamental question I ask. My view is, yes, there's a process of thinking that's more likely to get you answers. There's an intelligent process for identifying where to play, how to win, and if we make choices of that sort, we will position ourselves in a way that gives us the opportunity to keep modifying that and enhancing it ahead of other people so that we do have an advantage over a sustained period. It's not the same advantage, right; it actually could be different sorts of advantages over time. So if you look over a 50-year period, it may actually be a whole bunch of different sorts of advantages. But it's because we have a practice of asking a set of questions that keeps us ahead of the game rather than simply reacting to changes.

The world isn't static. Strategy isn't static, but that doesn't mean there isn't a way of thinking about the fundamental questions that keeps you ahead of the competition.

CHAPTER 7

Where Strategy
Meets Society

By the second half of the 1990s, business was undergoing a radical transformation courtesy of the Internet. The dot-com boom was under way, and management experts were reassessing the fundamental rules of business. It was no longer necessary to be profitable, it seemed. A better strategy, for the owners at least, was to load up with investment funds, embark on a mad dash for "eyeballs," and then cash in with an initial public offering (IPO), passing the long-term risk on to another investor. This was strategy but not as we had previously known it. It was the strategy of cyber-exploration. The closest parallel perhaps was when wealthy royal patrons in the fifteenth century would invest in nautical explorers who promised a lucrative future from the territories they discovered. As the valuation of small start-ups defied gravity, there were few people in business who did not caught up in dot-com fever.

But while management experts were pondering new business models, clicks and bricks, and burn rates, some strategists were turning their attention to another contributor to corporate success. A firm's interaction with the market, both internally and externally, had been well observed in connection with strategic management. Less studied, however, were the myriad nonmarket interactions and factors that influenced a company's success.

In 1995, the *California Management Review* published an article, "Integrated Strategy: Market and Non-Market Components," by the economist and Stanford University professor David P. Baron. It argued that effective strategic management must encompass both market and nonmarket strategy. In making his argument, Baron drew on a long line of academic thought that included the work of the economist Joseph Shister in the 1940s and also that of David Yoffie, Marianne Jennings, Frank Shipper, Alfred Marcus, Allen Kaufman, David R. Beam, Lee Preston, and James Post, among others. It was a line others would also follow, notably David Bach, former head of the Centre for Nonmarket Strategy at Spain's IE Business School and subsequently at the Yale School of Management.

The logic was compelling then and is even more so now. There is a substantial nonmarket component to any business environment. *Nonmarket* means any activity that is not based on or directly driven by market forces. The nonmarket space provides the social and political context in which all businesses have to operate. There is and has always been a nuanced negotiation between the two spheres that legitimizes and defines any firm's license to operate. The patterns and actions that take place in the nonmarket sphere affect an organization's ability to create value by increasing its overall performance.

Baron defines the nonmarket environment as including "those interactions that are intermediated by the public, stakeholders, government, the media, and public institutions." This is a very different environment from the market, where interactions tend to be voluntary and involve economic transactions and are intermediated by markets or private agreements.

In the nonmarket space, notes Baron, characteristics such as majority rule, due process, broad enfranchisement, and collective action are important. Interactions may be voluntary, such as a firm lobbying government departments, but are often involuntary, such as government legislation and regulations and product and service boycotts by pressure groups.

The I Test

In Baron's view, four Is characterize the nonmarket environment. *Issues* are what nonmarket strategies address, revising legislation, for example. *Institutions* such as governments, government departments, and regulatory bodies deal with nonmarket issues. *Interests* are individuals and groups involved in issues. Regulation of energy markets, for example, would involve energy companies, activist groups, consumers, manufacturers and suppliers, and the media. *Information* is what the interested parties know that is relevant to the nonmarket issue.

Whereas traditional business strategy is concerned with how to position the firm optimally in the face of market forces, nonmarket strategy is all about positioning the firm beneficially in the face of nonmarket forces.

Nonmarket strategy is more important for firms when opportunities to create value are controlled by nonmarket institutions such as governments. This is the case for firms operating in highly regulated business sectors such as biotechnology and medical devices, for example. Equally, nonmarket strategy assumes greater importance in businesses in areas where activist action is more prevalent, such as the metals and mining and oil and gas sectors. Today, too, with supply chains extending around the world, increasing numbers of firms are discovering that they are affected by the actions of pressure groups.

Baron argues that nonmarket strategies should be integrated with market strategies to create competitive advantage or defend a market position. He uses a number of cases to illustrate the point, demonstrating how a traditional Porter's five forces strategic approach, for example, can be complemented by nonmarket strategy to help Toys R Us globalize its business.

Deploying nonmarket strategy can help firms in number of ways, Baron asserts. For example, nonmarket strategies can be used to defend against rivals, create new market opportunities and defend against new entrants and substitutes, and address threats arising from the bargaining power of suppliers and buyers such as consumer product boycotts.

Firms may also adopt a competencies-based approach to nonmarket strategy, focusing on improving nonmarket competencies. For instance, that might mean building expertise in dealing with the government, media, and public and interest and activist groups. This entails understanding how key regulatory frameworks function, how policy-making decisions are shaped, and who is involved in formulating them.

Developing personal a relationship with key nonmarket individuals is particularly useful as these kinds of relationships are difficult assets for rivals to replicate. And unlike commercial market situations, antitrust rules do not generally preclude firms from working together through industry alliances and grouping to achieve nonmarket ends. Thus, these types of firm-to-firm relationship can be very valuable nonmarket mechanisms for obtaining competitive advantage.

Creating a strong reputation for responsible behavior with respect to nonmarket issues is also a common component of nonmarket strategies. Having a good reputation can help with regulatory dealings as well as sitting well with the public.

Where Baron led in his consideration of the way a complex web of social and political influences and institutions can exert a powerful force on the behavior and reputation of firms, others have followed. Indeed, the phrase *nonmarket forces* has become a useful term to describe an increasingly important set of strategic levers and stakeholder relationships.

Making Nonmarket Strategies Work

One of those making an important contribution in the field has been Yale's David Bach. With David Allen, dean of the faculty of management and law at the University of Surrey in the United Kingdom, Bach wrote an influential article in the *Sloan Management Review*, "What Every CEO Needs to Know About Nonmarket Strategy."

According to Bach and Allen, "Nonmarket strategy starts with a simple, dual premise—first, that issues and actors 'beyond the market' increasingly affect the bottom line, and, second, that they can be managed just as strategically as conventional 'core business' activities within markets. The challenge for CEOs and their leadership teams is one of simultaneous separation and integration. To successfully manage beyond the market, executives must recognize the important differences between the firm's market and nonmarket environments but then take an integrated, coherent and strategic approach to both arenas. This is the key to turning perceived 'nonbusiness' issues into strategic opportunities and thereby building sustainable competitive advantage."

Bach and Allen discuss a number of facets of nonmarket strategy. They address the role of globalization as a catalyst for nonmarket strategy development, for example. There are, say Bach and Allen, four factors linked to globalization that are driving nonmarket strategy. The first is that globalization means that companies have to address multiple audiences across continents and countries and thus navigate many nonmarket environments that often reflect markedly different social and political values.

Second, as Bach and Allen point out, it is not just business that is becoming global but also the influence of nongovernmental organizations (NGOs) and activists. Using social media and other modern communications technologies, activists can respond quickly, reporting events wherever they occur within hours and bringing them to the attention of consumers around the world.

Third, doing business around the globe means more market opportunities, but it also means being exposed to many regulatory environments, regional, national, and international. Governments have created many more regulatory agencies, and regulatory frameworks are far from uniform.

The fourth factor is that greater globalization has led to increased market competition. When organizations routinely use outsourcing to lower costs and fragment their value chains across the world, finding a competitive edge proves ever more difficult. Understandably, organizations are looking beyond market strategy to nonmarket strategy to capture that competitive advantage.

With the increasing importance of nonmarket strategy, say Bach and Allen, it is vital that executives come to grips with the main difference between managing in the market environment and managing in the nonmarket environment. For example, nonmarkets are not as predictable or uniform as markets. They vary in many ways: in regulations and policies and in public attitudes and responses to events. Exchanges in a nonmarket environment are primarily concerned with information rather than money, and unlike money, information is very context-specific.

Alliances are often the way to get things done in nonmarket environment. So although competition does exist, in terms of gaining access to policy makers, for example, firms need to be adept at collaboration to achieve nonmarket strategic goals.

In the market environment, flexibility is often a desirable attribute. Firms can adopt multiple positions and wait to see which develop the most promisingly. However, that is not a wise strategy to adopt in a nonmarket environment where consistency and long-term commitment are viewed as desirable attitudes. Taking multiple positions on social issues such as the use of sweatshops or obesity, for example, and then waiting to see which proves the most popular is unlikely to prove popular or successful.

A last significant difference, suggest Bach and Allen, is that values are very important in the nonmarket environment and should permeate any nonmarket strategy. Creating value, the fundamental aim of market competition, is less relevant in a nonmarket situation.

Breaking New Ground

Other thinkers are also breaking new ground in the nonmarket strategy movement. The head of the strategy and international business group at Warwick Business School and a professor of strategic management, Kamel Mellahi has been doing research that is especially concerned with the role of nonmarket strategy in emerging markets.

"It is widely accepted now that good connections with powerful political actors and institutions constitute a critical element of business success in emerging markets, where competition is shaped by nonmarket forces and institutional voids," he says. "This makes nonmarket strategy critical for firms operating in both developed and emerging economies."

One of the difficulties with nonmarket strategy lies with its definition, however. "Any concept that is defined in terms of what it is not—e.g., nonmarket—is problematic," says Kamel Mellahi. "But alternative descriptions such as CSR (corporate social responsibility) or lobbying fail to capture its full scope. Alternative terms have also failed to catch on. Perhaps it should be called 'social and political strategy.'"

As nonmarket strategy moves up the corporate agenda, with CEOs recognizing the increasing pressures they are under from political and social forces, the importance of a nonmarket response or strategy will increase. But this will bring challenges, too.

"Important as nonmarket forces are, there can be a dark side to nonmarket strategy. The value of political networks, in particular, changes over time," Mellahi says.

Take the case of foreign multinationals in the Chinese automobile industry. In the 1980s and 1990s, Shanghai Volkswagen

Automotive, the joint venture set up by Volkswagen, prospered while other joint ventures created by Peugeot and Chrysler struggled. In part, VW's success was due to the fact that non-market forces dominated the automotive industry in China and VW's nonmarket strategy was effective. In particular, its ability to embed itself in China's political networks paid dividends.

At that time, Chinese political institutions, as well as dictating which suppliers the joint venture could use, accounted for most of the passenger cars sold. VW's political ties and willingness to pay inflated prices to local suppliers enabled it to secure sales at a time when market forces were not the dominant factor.

But by 2000, market forces were asserting themselves as demand came increasingly from ordinary private buyers. At that time, VW's political embeddedness made it difficult for it to negotiate more competitive prices from local suppliers. As a result, VW's market share collapsed from 50 percent of passenger cars to 17 percent in just four years between 2001 and 2005.

"What the VW case illustrates is the need for firms to be flexible in their nonmarket strategies. What serves a company well at one time may actually become a disadvantage later," says Mellahi. "That's why it's critical that just as firms constantly review and revise their market strategies, they must also adopt a similar awareness and discipline with nonmarket strategy."

The Pious Prius

David Bach and David Allen also use an automotive example to demonstrate how nonmarket strategy can be successfully deployed. They point to the car manufacturer Toyota. The Japanese automaker saw the possibilities associated with hybrid cars relatively early, early enough for it to become a market leader. However, Toyota also stretched the competitive playing field beyond the market, playing its nonmarket strategy hand with consummate skill.

In California, the company successfully lobbied the local government to include its flagship Prius hybrid model in a program granting low-emissions vehicles access to the state's car pool lanes even when there was only a single occupant. Support from environmental groups made it easy for legislators to endorse the proposal, which cost the state of California next to nothing and burnished its environmental credentials.

Toyota gave its product a decisive competitive advantage with a minimum financial investment. It was impressive nonmarket maneuvering. Building on this success, the company next won Prius owners the right to park for free at public meters in Los Angeles and other cities. Through skillful nonmarket management that deftly complements the company's existing market strategy of selling the product primarily to upper-middle-class, environmentally conscious urban professionals, Toyota has reinforced its competitive advantage.

The Prius C was among the five finalists at the 2012 Los Angeles Auto Show for the 2013 Green Car of the Year, awarded by the *Green Car Journal*.

A greater challenge has been Toyota's management of the nonmarket aspects of recent product recalls. In 2009 and 2010, at a time when the company had just overtaken General Motors to become the largest car manufacturer in the world, Toyota faced a problem with accelerators sticking on some models. This led to a mass product recall. Initially, however, the matter was underplayed and caused significant public relations problems.

The case emphasizes the fact that nonmarket strategy is a holistic process that requires a firm's management to monitor its positioning among stakeholders, including the arena of public opinion.

As David Bach points out, however, "Few firms are prepared to do the hard work and commit long-term to developing an effective nonmarket strategy. Fewer still understand how to integrate market and nonmarket strategies to sustain competitive advantage."

Through the Bach Door

When we talked to David Bach, we asked him to explain the growing interest in nonmarket forces.

What is nonmarket strategy? Why is it important?
And why is it important now?
Nonmarket strategy is simply the idea that the business environment consists of more than just markets. There are the other stakeholders who bear directly on a company's ability to create and defend competitive advantage: governments, regulators, nongovernmental organizations, the media, and so forth. We can call these nonmarket actors, and they become increasingly important in terms of the influence that they have on a company.

Just as a firm strategically manages its market environment and comes up with a plan for creating competitive advantage, it should do the same for the nonmarket environment.

Can you illustrate the importance of nonmarket actors?

It varies a lot across industries. For example, there are some industries that really can't function without the important role taken by nonmarket actors. Take the pharmaceutical industry, for example. For a business model to work based around the development of proprietary blockbuster drugs, you need very strong intellectual property protection. For that you need a government. Also, drugs have a very important and elaborate approval system. The perspective on the industry held by political stakeholders is very important.

Pharmaceutical companies are now investing more in corporate social responsibility and reputation management. One reason is that they realize that the fallout from reputational problems, such as drugs that don't work well and pricing drugs so that people in developing countries can't access them, can ultimately be a fundamental challenge to their business and their business model, because it could potentially undermine public support for strong patent protection.

In the 1990s, Chiquita Brands sourced most of its bananas from Latin America; Europe was its biggest market. Meanwhile, the European Union changed its banana policies to favor non–Latin American suppliers. Chiquita missed this nonmarket event and suffered as a result. Dole, in contrast, one of the largest producers of fresh fruit and vegetables, tracked the workings of the commission, diversified its suppliers, and improved its business as a result.

Looking back, is it that organizations have ignored this area of strategy or that they have dealt with it but in a kind of ad hoc piecemeal way? Or that they didn't recognize the significance of it, or it's become kind of critical mass and now they have to recognize it?

I think it is a little bit of all of this. Senior executives know that politics and society matter to them. What they haven't really been very good at is thinking about this as naturally a part of the business environment and markets.

Companies are very comfortable with the idea that you can shape customers' expectations, erect entry barriers, change your relationship with suppliers, and mold your market environment. They are not so comfortable with the idea of trying to mold their social and political environment.

It sounds like what you're saying is that organizations have seen the nonmarket aspects of the environment as something that affected their business as opposed to something that they could proactively deal with.

I think that is exactly right. I mean, go back 30 years, and before Michael Porter strategic management was essentially about positioning yourself in an industry and the industry dynamics were taken as given, and there was very little that you could do about that. But then people started realizing that in fact you can do something to improve your competitiveness even in an unattractive industry, for example.

So companies have been doing things, but often in piecemeal fashion, different initiatives directed at different stakeholders. So you have your government affairs department, legal department, corporate social responsibility team, and corporate communications team, but they are all separate from one another, not really joined together by a common strategy and perhaps somewhat removed from the core corporate strategy process.

So how do we go about addressing nonmarket strategy in an organization?

We have a framework. Basically, the idea is that you look at six different questions when you analyze your nonmarket environment. What is the issue you're dealing with? Who are the actors who have a stake in this issue? What are the interests of those actors? In what arena did these actors meet, and does this issue get settled? What information moves the issue in this arena? What assets do you need in order to prevail?

It is very simple, but it does help you get the first assessment of what your nonmarket might look like. It helps you think more strategically about how to manage an issue and ultimately, as you start to manage different issues that affect you, start deliberately shaping the nonmarket environment.

Can you quickly run through the steps? What would we do to get from nothing to being in a position where we are able to take some action?

I don't think it's that complicated. Start off by asking what the strategy is for the market: how the company is positioned, how it is competing, what the product is, and the value proposition to customers. Based on that, think about what the critical social and political issues are and where their resolution one way or another is going to affect the ability of the company to create an appropriate value.

We're not talking about creating separate departments necessarily; we're talking about sensitizing the key executives in the organization to think about strategy, not to think just about market actors but to think consistently also about the nonmarket actors who have a role in this and what you could do to bring them to your side, influence their views, create alliances with them, and launch initiatives, all in support, ultimately, of the same goal, which is your competitiveness.

So there is no separate nonmarket strategy department?

If you create a big corporate bureaucracy, that doesn't help anybody. You want to sensitize your line managers and business unit managers to the fact that nonmarket actors and social and political forces actually matter a great deal for the company. Train them to pick up on potential social and political developments that could affect the company in the short, medium, and long term. Then have them work directly in the nonmarket environment or, quite likely, through the corporate support function, for example, to address some of those concerns.

What are the biggest mistakes companies make? What are the things managers shouldn't do that they need to be watching out for?

One big mistake is to think this is a silver bullet. It takes time to develop nonmarket relationships, to begin working with nongovernment organizations, to have a network of public officials whom you know and where you understand them but you also make sure that they understand you as a company.

Another mistake is that there is a misalignment between market and nonmarket. A lot of people are skeptical about companies dabbling in politics. When companies take political positions, people often sense ulterior motives. So it is really important to be consistent in what you do.

Is nonmarket strategy all about winners and losers, or can it be collaborative and cooperative as well?

Absolutely. There is a lot of cooperation here. In the nonmarket environment it is a lot about building coalitions, cultivating relationships, and slowly changing the environment in which you compete. But having said that, it doesn't mean that the nonmarket environment is all peace and harmony; this is a very competitive space. Different actors can compete for attention from key opinion leaders or policy makers, for example.

In terms of measurement and performance, how do you justify the time spent on this?

What most managers and senior executives agree on is that when you can do these things, the returns are vast. When you can avoid a piece of unfavorable legislation or influence a piece of legislation or use your market leadership to actually create standards around the product that you have designed that create entry barriers for the competition, the returns on this are usually considerable.

CHAPTER 8

Where Strategy Meets the World

Eventually, strategists inevitably feel cramped by coming up with neat strategies for corporations, however multinational they may be. They crave a bigger stage. Michael Porter has tackled strategy in the healthcare industry, notably in a series of articles coauthored with his Harvard colleague Mark Kramer. Porter has also squared the capitalist circle by showing how companies can combine their competitive instincts with social responsibility and other activities that although they are socially beneficial do not appear to contribute to shareholder value.

Perhaps Porter's most successful foray into other corners of the strategy world was his work on competition and countries. His 1990 book *The Competitive Advantage of Nations* must be ranked as one of the most ambitious books of our times. At its heart was a radical new perspective on the role and *raison d'être* of nations. Porter charted the transformation of nations from being military powerhouses to being economic units whose competitiveness is the key to power and influence.

The questions Porter sought to answer were familiar. Building on the ideas in his previous books, he examined what makes a nation's firms and industries competitive in global markets and what propels a whole nation's economy to advance. "Why are firms based in a particular nation able to create and sustain competitive advantage against the world's best competitors in a particular field? And why is one nation often the home for so many of an industry's world leaders?" he asked. "Why is tiny Switzerland the home base for international leaders in pharmaceuticals, chocolate and trading? Why are leaders in heavy trucks and mining equipment based in Sweden?"

Although he drew on previous concepts and work, Porter was starting over, returning to first principles. "The principal economic goal of a nation is to produce a high and rising standard of living for its citizens. The ability to do so depends not on the amorphous notion of 'competitiveness' but on the productivity with which a nation's resources (labor and capital) are employed," he wrote. "Productivity is the prime determinant in the long run of a nation's standard of living." Some might argue that this was a misguided conclusion, and some nations have notably begun to question the basis of the way they measure success, investigating alternatives to gross domestic product (GDP) such as happiness and well-being.

Far from championing the end of the nation-state, as some commentators did, against a backdrop of the inexorable globalization of business, Porter came to different conclusions. He identified a central paradox.

Companies and industries have become globalized and more international in their scope and aspirations than ever before. This, on the surface at least, would appear to suggest that the nation has lost its role in the international success of its firms. But that was not what Porter's research showed.

"Companies, at first glance, seem to have transcended countries. Yet what I have learned in this study contradicts this conclusion," said Porter. "While globalization of competition might appear to make the nation less important, instead it seems to make it more so. With fewer impediments to trade to shelter uncompetitive domestic firms and industries, the home nation takes on growing significance because it is the source of the skills and technology that underpin competitive advantage."

Porter also laid down a challenge, perhaps to himself, to solve another perennial mystery: "Much is known about what competitive advantage is and how particular actions create or destroy it. Much else is known about why a company makes good choices instead of bad choices in seeking bases for competitive advantage, and why some firms are more aggressive in pursuing them." Porter's conclusion was that it is the intensity of domestic competition that often fuels success on a global stage.

To make sense of the dynamics behind national or regional strength in a particular industry, Porter developed the national "diamond." This is made up of four (not five) forces:

1. **Factor conditions.** These once would have included natural resources and plentiful supplies of labor; now they embrace data communications, university research, and

the availability of scientists, engineers, or experts in a particular field.

2. **Demand conditions.** If there is strong national demand for a product or service, this can give the industry a head start in global competition. The United States, for example, is ahead in health services because of heavy national demand.

3. **Related and supporting industries.** Industries that are strong in a particular country are often surrounded by successful related industries.

4. **Firm strategy, structure, and rivalry.** Domestic competition fuels growth and competitive strength.

Hypercompetitive Capitalism

Richard D'Aveni is another thinker who has continued to find new facets of strategy to explore. Most recently, in his 2012 book *Strategic Capitalism*, he has scaled up the target of his strategic analysis. Like Porter before him and a number of other strategists, D'Aveni eventually shifted his unit of analysis from business or firm to government and nation and ultimately to entire economic systems. Thus, in this book he is concerned with hypercompetition between various forms of capitalism and the economic power struggle between nations and economic power blocs. In particular, D'Aveni is interested in the different models of capitalism being pursued by the United States and China.

The word *iconoclast* is overused, but not in the case of Richard D'Aveni. D'Aveni is a contrarian. One of the reasons we like his work is that he looks at the world differently and dares to challenge orthodoxy. His analysis is controversial. It is as provocative as it is refreshingly unflinching.

D'Aveni notes that a constant stream of headlines from China indicate that corporate America is under attack. When we talked to him, he pointed to two recent examples: the Bo Xilai scandal, a story that illustrated how business interests in China are tied up with affairs of the state, and the fact that the Fed had allowed three state-owned Chinese banks to move into U.S. markets.

Why do these stories resonate for you?

Because they illustrate two profoundly worrying trends. The former shows how Chinese business is closely entwined with the machinations of Chinese politics and corruption. The latter because America is happy to open its markets—in this case the banking market—to Chinese competitors that may serve the government of China, its politics, and its corruption. Together these two trends constitute the biggest threat to U.S. national interests in decades.

Today we face a turning point in American history, a time requiring reinvention. Even as the job market picks up temporarily, we are warned of a "new normal": an economy where good jobs are disappearing overseas and where wage averages are depressed by foreign competition. Tepid growth. Unstable careers. Fewer opportunities. Dependence on foreign imports for survival. Even the loss of America's position as the leader of the global economy is a possibility.

Where does the threat to the American economic power base come from?

Underlying the new normal are two sources: China's aggressive economic growth and corporate America's docile response.

China has emerged from a meager capitalist adolescence to vibrant adulthood. It has mastered manufacturing so quickly that even companies as American as Apple now make almost everything in Chinese plants. China has acted so aggressively to build its manufacturing enterprises that it has taken over 2 million American jobs in the last decade. It has gained such speed that if current growth rates continue, its economy will surpass that of the United States before 2030. Meanwhile, the U.S. economy stagnates and becomes infiltrated by Chinese firms that are instruments of a nonelected, nondemocratic power seeking to supplant the United States as the world leader.

But there are alternative explanations for the current American ills.

Yes; some commentators point to an aging population, for example, or technological unemployment: the tendency for ICT [information and communications technology] and other technologies to replace human labor. But my focus is on the impact of China's system of capitalism on U.S. competitiveness.

What we are witnessing, in my view, is an escalation from competition between corporations to competition between nations. The struggle between

China and the United States amounts to the opening moves of a capitalist cold war.

With the rise of the new economic powerhouses, especially China, we are seeing a new form of capitalism where states compete against other states or, more accurately, their forms of capitalism compete with each other for economic success.

The famous economist Joseph Schumpeter argued that the forces of creative destruction are integral to the efficient working of a capitalist system. Schumpeter's ideas are widely accepted. I am arguing that those same forces work on the system itself, so that a better-adapted form of capitalism will eventually destroy or displace the incumbent system. This dynamic process is at work around the world.

Is this hypercompetition between nations?

Yes, absolutely. In the 1990s, I coined the term *hypercompetition* to describe a situation where companies no longer enjoy sustainable competitive advantages and compete by continuously disrupting rivals. My research indicates that we are entering an era of economic hypercompetition between nations.

What does that mean in practical terms?

It comprises a series of actions by rival nations seeking to tilt the playing field to their advantage, in effect to set the rules of competition. It also includes moves and countermoves to disrupt or undermine the form of capitalism used by rivals. We have seen it before.

In the 1970s and 1980s, for example, corporate Japan developed a form of managed capitalism that featured domestic industry groups called *keiretsu*[1] and informal *zaibatsu*[2] (which were formally outlawed after World War II). They did not seek to maximize corporate profits in the short run; they sought to maximize employment in Japan and reinvestment in the long-term growth of the groups. It was capitalism, but not as we knew it in the United States.

Japanese companies took advantage of American complacency by disrupting U.S. manufacturing industries, especially in autos, electronics, machine tools, and steel. For a time, it looked as if the Japanese economic juggernaut would overtake the United States, but in the end a combination of factors meant that Japan's growth stalled.

China now poses a more potent threat. My research confirms that China is now a "hypercompetitor." Corporate China in close collaboration with the Chinese government has taken the same approach as Japan with managed capitalism. But it has added the weight of its larger population, more state control of financing and labor practices, a neomercantilist approach, speedy nondemocratic decision-making processes, and its willingness to play tough with foreign suppliers and buyers. That has brought the United States into a growing economic confrontation.

So, what can American and other Western companies do to raise their game?

Now is not the time to rely on ideological or theory-based ideas that encapsulate what *used* to work. Most ideologies and theories are not appropriate anymore. They freeze our thinking, paralyze our ability to adjust, and doom American companies to continued deadlock and decline. Only a fool continues doing the same thing and expects different results.

The time has come for real leadership. An honest debate about the situation can help the United States break out of its rigid stance. The simple fact is that by continuing to promote free trade, we are damaging U.S. competitiveness.

In *Strategic Capitalism*, I urge American business leaders to look at the future strategically and to craft a strategy for winning over the long term. It does not promote ideology, whether from the left, right, or center. It promotes pragmatic thinking that comes from anyone with good ideas.

Most important of all, it urges American business leaders to return to what made the United States an economic colossus: entrepreneurial dynamism and exporting combined with government R&D and barriers to entry for foreign firms. The greatest American industries have been created and sustained in this manner: aerospace, agriculture, defense, pharmaceuticals, and many more. Firms acting alone cannot compete with China's new version of capitalism. American firms must work together with the government to outmaneuver or match China's system.

The simple fact is that China's version of capitalism is allowing it to grow much faster than the United States is, albeit from a much lower base.

What can business leaders do?

It is time for American business leaders to add their voices to the debate. It is only by their making themselves heard and taking decisive action that the United States can avert economic decline. I believe there are five lessons that U.S. corporations need to learn and learn quickly.

First and foremost, they must break the China taboo. The first lesson for American business leaders is to have the courage to speak out about the difficulties of doing business in China. Some of us recall the stand that people such as Andy Grove at Intel and other corporate leaders took when they perceived that the Japanese domestic market was closed to them. Yet most of today's CEOs—and I've talked to hundreds of them—will simply not go on record criticizing China. They tell me regularly that they don't know what to do. They are damned if they enter China due to the risk and fear of becoming controlled by the Chinese government, and they are damned if they don't due to the size and growth of Chinese markets and their potential to create shareholder wealth. But they wouldn't dream of starting a public conversation about the bind they are in, because that might decrease their stock price or encourage Chinese retaliation. The subject is taboo.

Second, they should practice corporate patriotism. The second lesson is the need to take a more patriotic view of business. At present, short-termism (largely as a result of pressure from Wall Street) means that business decisions are based on maximizing shareholder return regardless of the impact on the national economy. As a result, the location of manufacturing plants and other investment decisions are based on making short-term profits even when they damage the competitiveness of the U.S. economy in the long run.

Millions of U.S. jobs have been exported to China and other countries as a result. Yet the reality is that upward wage pressure in China means that it is no longer the cheap source of labor it once was, and that wage pressure will only increase. It is time to repatriate U.S. manufacturing for national strategic and business reasons. (This links to the fourth lesson.)

The third imperative is to recognize that free trade comes at a price. Many people argue in favor of market efficiency and opening up the U.S. domestic market, but this is damaging to American businesses. Market efficiency drives down prices, which may be good for consumers in the short run but is at the expense of profits. Falling profits mean that U.S. businesses have less money to invest in R&D and training for their workers. This affects American competitiveness, forcing us to compete on cost alone. It ignores the fact that the U.S. market is a mature market and should be a source of competitive advantage to domestic companies. Some will see this as protectionism, but I disagree. I believe that American business leaders need to recognize and exploit their home advantages, not allow them to be negotiated away in the name of some moribund economic ideology.

Fourth, beware of your China exposure. Many U.S. companies are pursuing expansion plans in China with something approaching strategic abandon. But those plans will turn around and bite them in the next few years. Very few U.S. companies will be able to build profitable businesses in China. What we are currently witnessing is the equivalent of a gold rush. What these companies can see is an explosion of growth in the Chinese domestic market, but what few have fully understood is that the Chinese version of capitalism will squeeze out Western interests as soon as they become profitable.

It is true that a few U.S. companies are operating profitably in China at present, but the vast majority are banking on the idea that they will reap the benefits later, and many have built that expectation into their financial projections. In the next few years, Wall Street will start asking where the beef is and will be disappointed. Smart business leaders will anticipate this backlash and rethink their China exposure. They will have contingency plans to cover the holes in their growth plans when profits from China fail to materialize and to withdraw their assets at short notice if necessary in the event of political unrest or government interference.

Finally, rethink your China strategy. Many American CEOs can see the problems in China but are under pressure from Wall Street to pursue the China mirage. One exception is Jeff Immelt at GE, who has criticized China as hostile to multinationals and said that he is deemphasizing China in GE's growth plans. Could this be the beginning of a corporate exodus? I hope so. GE's decision to bring back to Louisville, Kentucky, hundreds of jobs in its domestic appliances business that had been outsourced to Mexico and China is a sign that Immelt gets it.

For GE, the balance of employment had been shifting away from the United States. At the end of 2011, 131,000 of its 301,000 staff were based in the United States. Since 2009, though, it has announced plans to create 13,500 new U.S. jobs, 11,000 in manufacturing. Other companies should do the same thing.

The World of Strategy

Another thinker challenging received wisdom about the world is Pankaj Ghemawat. Ghemawat is the Anselmo Rubiralta Professor of Global Strategy at IESE Business School in Spain. Before that he was the youngest full professor ever appointed at Harvard Business School.

Best known for his work on globalization, Ghemawat has written books that include *Games Businesses Play: Cases and Models* (1997), *Creating Value Through International Strategy* (2005), *Redefining Global Strategy: Crossing Borders in a World*

Where Differences Still Matter (2007), and *Strategy and the Business Landscape* (2009).

In *World 3.0: Global Prosperity and How to Achieve It* (2011), Ghemawat examines globalization and the assumptions made about it. He refutes the idea that there is a single global economy, the central premise of Thomas Friedman's 2006 book *The World Is Flat*. Instead, he argues, on the basis of various economic measures and indicators, that nations are much more disconnected than we imagine. We live, he says, in a world that is semiglobalized at best.

Regional differences exist and matter, argues Ghemawat, and the unevenness and differences that exist from region to region are a potential source of commercial advantage.

Your book is called World 3.0. *What was wrong with* World 1.0 *and* 2.0—*and* 0.0 *for that matter?*

Well, let's start with World 1.0. When I was in graduate school, I had a whole course in macroeconomics from Martin Feldstein, and what he told us on the last day of the course was, Well, it's great that you've absorbed all these models, but these are all closed economy models, and if you want to take advanced macroeconomics, that's a whole different kettle of fish. So that to me is World 1.0, recognizing that there are cross-border interactions but still pretending that we can more or less grasp reality by thinking of countries as self-contained.

We then move into World 2.0?

World 2.0 is actually still with us. This is the belief that is the polar opposite of World 1.0, which is that national borders don't matter at all and that cross-border integration is nearly complete.

That's the Tom Friedman view that the world is flat?

I ran a survey recently on the *Harvard Business Review* web platform giving people three different world-views that they could sign up for, and 62 percent of the respondents went for Tom Friedman's characterization of a world in which borders don't matter, distance is irrelevant, languages have no effect, and so forth.

You argue that the world isn't as flat as Friedman would have us believe.

Right. I think most people would recognize that there are still some barriers, but it's amazing to me how many people regard them as just noise or trivial as witness the responses to the *HBR* survey I mentioned. So what I'd like to do is get people to focus on countries of particular interest to them and try to really understand the structure of those countries' international economic relationships. So take the United States, for example.

The largest bilateral trading partner of the United States isn't China; it's Canada. Canada is also the largest supplier of oil to the United States. Canada also ranks in the top two countries in terms of destinations for U.S. citizens placing phone calls. Yet Canada is certainly not the second largest economy in the world.

International phone calls actually account for only 2 percent of total phone calls, which is shocking to people who believe in a globalized world.

The basic point is that these levels of cross-border interactions are much lower than what you would expect in a fully integrated world and are much lower than what people tend to guess. This suggests that it's important to recalibrate and start with an accurate picture of how integrated we actually are, and that's what I try and present in *World 3.0*. So we are actually in a state of semiglobalization. What you find is that only 10 to 25 percent of most types of economic activity is actually international. Even more surprisingly, the lion's share of that activity is between countries that are similar: share borders, belong to the same trading bloc, speak the same language, or have colonial ties. As distances and differences between countries increase, their economic interactions typically decrease.

Yet a lot of people are very frightened of globalization. Why are people so scared of it?

I think it goes back to exaggerations about how globalized we actually are. If you're proglobalization, this is dangerous because it suggests to you that there's no further room for increases in integration to yield any benefits. And if you're antiglobalization, in a 100 percent globalized world, it's plausible to blame everything on globalization. So many of the fears that antiglobalizers have about globalization are fueled by the same kinds of misconceptions that lead even proglobalizers to overlook the gains from additional integration.

So people are fearful about losing their jobs, fearful about the poorer parts of the world being exploited by the richer parts of the world, and all these sorts of things, but what you're saying is that those fears are overblown.

There are some real issues here. I spend seven chapters in my book dealing with various kinds of market failures and fears that people have and whether globalization makes them better or worse off, and I think that for some of these failures and fears you can actually see globalization ameliorating rather than aggravating things. For others of these failures and fears, although globalization may play a role, 10 to 20 percent globalization plays a very different role from what one might expect 100 percent globalization to play.

A tension within the book—in fact, it's the central tension in the book—is between this process of globalization or international integration, if you like, between economies and the notion of regulation and reining it back and, to some extent, protectionism. Can that tension be resolved?

At the end of the day, there are some tensions, but I think the tensions do get relaxed if you've recognized how limited current levels of globalization are. Let me give you an example. What people in poor countries in particular worry about the most is food prices. And in fact I started writing this book in response to the international rice crisis in 2007–2008, when international rice prices tripled. To many people then and to many people now, this is an argument for shutting down international trade in rice.

But when you realize that only 5 percent of the rice that is produced in the world is traded internationally, you realize that anything that happens on the supply side or anything that's happening on the demand side gets loaded onto that 5 percent. So the way to deal with that is not to reduce that 5 percent to 2 percent or 1 percent; it's to increase the fraction that's traded globally. So increasing integration in this instance would actually help.

You asked about regulation, and rice is a good illustration that although increased integration can in this instance help reduce volatility, it probably isn't sufficient because it's neither politically nor ethically justifiable to let people starve if they can't afford rice at the prices that it settles down at. So, at the end of the day, I have a message that involves certainly relying on integration as the prime engine of moving the global economy forward but recognizing that in some circumstances we will need some regulation.

What about a situation such as the production of rare earths, a commodity being used in a lot of electronic and computer devices. People point to the fact that

China appears to have a global monopoly. What's the situation there?

Well, certainly China has approximately 95 percent of rare earths production. This is another kind of market failure that people worry about, small numbers or, in its extreme form, monopoly. And monopolies are bad, but it's hard to say we're the United States or we're the United Kingdom; we should shut ourselves off from the world in response to this problem. It's much more efficient to do what's being done and help other countries that have reserves, such as Vietnam, develop those sources of rare earths.

So we still have a lot of monopolies or oligopolies, particularly in commodity sectors, and the answer is not to shut oneself off from the rest of the world. Because with something like rare earths, if you don't have those reserves, there is no possibility of developing them yourself. It's about trying to build up a more robust supply chain that involves more integration with more countries rather than turning one's back on the world.

One of the things we really like about the book is that it talks about how we can respond as individuals and it recognizes that we are individual units of analysis in this globalized world. We particularly like the notion of the rooted cosmopolitan. Can you talk about that a little?

Well, the rooted cosmopolitan is a little bit of an analogue of the country example that I was just using.

Where you're located affects what's close and what's far. So rooted cosmopolitans recognize that certain experiences and certain peoples are much more approximate to themselves. A rooted cosmopolitan does not attempt this rootless cosmopolitan idea of trying to pretend that one cares equally about everything that's happening everywhere in the world. A rooted cosmopolitan just realizes that we all have certain roots and that that's important to figuring out what we should try to do and whom we should try to do it with.

So is this a more realistic notion than urging people to suddenly become global citizens, which we have failed to take on board?

That's right, and my favorite example of that is this notion of looking at the reality versus some of the rhetoric around global citizens. People who have the concept of universal cosmopolitans as opposed to rooted cosmopolitans suggest to us that we should care equally about people halfway around the world as we do about our neighbors. But I think both psychologically and economically that's unrealistic. What I emphasize instead in my book is that if you look at how much, for instance, the governments of rich countries spend on domestic poor versus foreign poor, the ratio is roughly 30,000 to 1. And what we're talking about, let's say the real targets for increasing aid to developing countries, is bringing that ratio down from 30,000 to 1 to 15,000 to 1. That strikes me as a much more realistic proposition than simply saying okay, that ratio has to go to 1 to 1, which is not going to happen this century or probably the next century.

Do we need a new sort of regulation? Is it time now for supernational regulation that would operate across national borders?

Governmental bandwidth is always scarce, and I think, especially given how old our multilateral institutions are, that's the scarcest kind of governmental bandwidth imaginable. So another thing that I try to do in the book is articulate which kinds of problems can be regulated locally and which few problems absolutely do require multilateral coordination and multilateral regulation. Take the problems associated with pollution, for instance. Most pollutants that have very short radii operate over very short distances, and so local or national regulation works perfectly well. For pollutants with intermediate ranges, say, carbon dioxide or acid rain, having to do with sulfuric acid being deposited by rain, regional solutions can work and regional solutions have in fact worked. And then of course the hardest kind of problem is something like carbon dioxide in global warming, which isn't distance-sensitive, and there we do need multilateral coordination. But rather than say that everything should be a multilateral solution, I try to specify in what kinds of cases multilateral coordination is really required because that's the kind of coordination that seems hardest to achieve.

Can we put a reverse gear on globalization, on integration? Can you actually go backward? Is this a realistic proposition?

Well, let's start with the problems in the eurozone. I think the problems in the eurozone, and it's a similar set of problems with the Schengen Area without border controls, was a focus on just administrative barriers between countries and the very naive notion that if you got rid of those administrative barriers, all other problems would be taken care of and perfect integration would result. Having a common currency did not eliminate the economic differences among different parts of Europe in terms of productivity, growth rates, willingness to work long hours, and so forth.

Similarly, eliminating border controls did not eliminate the cultural prejudices that people in different parts of Europe have about people from other parts of Europe. So one of the things that have to happen is recognizing that there are actually many barriers to cross-border integration and that unbalanced integration is not the way to go. Having said that, I am very worried that steps backward in terms of revocation of the Schengen accords or ejecting Greece from the common currency represent the first significant reversals of a process that's been under way in Europe for the last 50-plus years. It's a process that's proceeded in fits and starts, but compared to the original vision that the founders of the European Coal and Steel Community had, it has probably

We talked about false assumptions and the fears that globalization creates. Are you optimistic about the future of this globalization project?

I'm very optimistic about the medium to long run. In the short run we have a major crisis in public finances, particularly in the developed world, and it has different manifestations on different sides of the Atlantic. We've talked about the eurozone problems, but we haven't talked about the problems in the United States with fiscal imbalances and inability to agree on mechanisms to bring the economy back into balance.

Well, interestingly, government debt seems to be one of the most effectively globalized commodities.

It does seem to be more globalized than some other commodities, and I remember calculating some data before the crisis; on a weighted average basis, somewhere between 45 and 55 percent of holdings of government debt were external. I'd add two things to that. First, that's still very far from 80 to 100 percent. Second, given what we've been seeing, there is a very rapid reduction in that figure. And so if you look right now at, for instance, Greece's external obligations, 90 percent of Greece's external obligations, if you focus on debt to banks, are to banks in the eurozone; that's why it's a European problem.

In contrast, if you look at U.S. banks' exposure to the eurozone problems, with the exception of Ireland, which historically has been close to the United States for a number of different reasons—

geographically, ethnically, and so on—and where U.S. banks' exposure does amount to something like 10 or 11 percent of Ireland's total foreign debt, for the other PIGS [Portugal, Italy, Greece, and Spain] countries it's 2, 4, or 5 percent. And so there's a reason why it's the Europeans who have been so focused on solving the problem in Greece because not only are international relationships limited, but those international interactions that do take place in our world mostly occur between countries that are close to each other culturally, geographically, economically, and so forth.

A Final Word

Just as Henry Mintzberg warns of the dangers of disconnecting strategy from business reality, Richard Rumelt points to the perils of bad strategy over good strategy. Rumelt has been described as the "strategist's strategist." It is fitting, then, that he rounds out our tour of strategy.

Rumelt holds the Harry and Elsa Kunin Chair in Business and Society at UCLA Anderson School of Management. He is best known for his work on corporate strategy, and his research has covered corporate diversification strategy and sustainable advantage and more recently industry transitions and the evolution of complex industries. He has authored or coauthored numerous business publications, including three books: *Strategy, Structure, and Economic Performance* (1974), *Fundamental Issues in Strategy* (1994), and *Good Strategy/Bad Strategy* (2011).

In the latter book, Rumelt sets out to explain "the logic of good strategy and the sources of power that talented strategists have tapped." This includes a detailed discussion about competitive advantage, how to strengthen it, how to exploit inertia, and riding waves of change. It also provides an insight into what constitutes bad strategy.

The book opens with a brief account of Admiral Horatio Nelson's naval victory at the Battle of Trafalgar in 1805, when a British fleet consisting of 27 ships defeated the combined forces of the French and Spanish, which numbered 33 ships. Nelson won the day by adopting an unconventional strategy. Flouting the naval convention of the time, he divided his smaller fleet into two columns and sailed them perpendicularly into the enemy fleet to cut the Franco-Spanish line.

Nelson knew that his lead ships would be vulnerable to Franco-Spanish guns until they could close on the opposing fleet. He gambled that the less-well-trained enemy gunners would not be able to capitalize on their advantage. He was proved right. The French and Spanish cannons were not able to compensate for the heavy swell and missed their opportunity to sink the British ships while they could not return fire. Once the battle was joined, the superiority of the British seamanship was decisive. The French and Spanish lost 22 ships, and the British lost none. This, as Rumelt points out, is an example of a good strategy.

"Nelson's challenge was that he was outnumbered. His strategy was to risk his lead ships in order to break the coherence of his enemy's fleet. With coherence lost, he judged, the more experienced English captains would come out on top in the ensuing melee. Good strategy almost always looks this simple and obvious and does not take a thick deck of PowerPoint slides to explain. It does not pop out of some 'strategic management' tool, matrix, chart, triangle, or fill-in-the-blanks scheme. Instead, a talented leader identifies the one or two critical issues in the situation—the pivot points that can multiply the effectiveness of effort—and then focuses and concentrates action and resources on them.

"Despite the roar of voices wanting to equate strategy with ambition, leadership, 'vision,' planning, or the economic logic of competition, strategy is none of these. The core of strategy work is always the same: discovering the critical factors in a situation and designing a way of coordinating and focusing actions to deal with those factors."

Rumelt provides a timely reminder that strategy is all about matching the resources at your disposal to a specific situation or context and using them in unexpected ways to create an advantage or overcome a disadvantage. Usually, that involves using strengths against weaknesses. But a good strategy also has a coherence of design that minimizes risks and maximizes the chances of success. In short, a good strategy is a joined-up strategy. Leaders must appraise the situation facing the organization and find a way to overcome the obstacles to reach objectives. Sometimes that requires them to take a risk. But it should always be a calculated risk and one that is taken without leaving the organization unnecessarily exposed or vulnerable.

As Rumelt explains: "A leader's most important responsibility is identifying the biggest challenges to forward progress and devising a coherent approach to overcoming them. In contexts ranging from corporate direction to national security, strategy matters. Yet we have become so accustomed to strategy as exhortation that we hardly blink an eye when a leader spouts slogans and announces high-sounding goals, calling the mixture a "'strategy.'"

He contrasts Nelson's high-risk strategy with that of Lehman Brothers. By 2006, the U.S. property market had peaked. A rise in the Fed's interest rates led to an increase in foreclosures. Lehman CEO Richard Fuld's strategic response was a strategy of continuing to gain market share by growing faster than its competitors. To do so Lehman would increase its "risk appetite," as Wall Street put it. It would take on the deals that other banks were rejecting. Unfortunately, this was not a rounded strategy; it lacked a response to the problems of taking on greater risk. Without this it was little more than blind ambition and a very bad strategy indeed.

"Operating with only 3 percent equity, and much of its debt supplied on a very short-term basis, this policy should have been accompanied by clever ways of mitigating the increased risk," observes Rumelt. "A good strategy recognizes the nature of the challenge and offers a way of surmounting it. Simply being ambitious is not a strategy. In 2008, Lehman Brothers ended its 158 years as an investment bank with a crash that sent the global financial system into a tailspin. Here, the consequences of bad strategy were disastrous for Lehman, the United States, and the world."

Rumelt's work offers a cautionary tale for all strategists. There are two dimensions, he says, to a good strategy.

Having a coherent strategy—one that coordinates policies and actions. A good strategy doesn't just draw on existing strength; it creates strength through the coherence of its design. Most organizations of any size don't do this. Rather, they pursue multiple objectives that are unconnected with one another or, worse, that conflict with one another.

"The creation of new strengths through subtle shifts in viewpoint. An insightful reframing of a competitive situation can create whole new patterns of advantage and weakness. The most powerful strategies arise from such game-changing insights."

And bad strategy? According to Rumelt, that has four hallmarks which should set alarm bells ringing:

1. Failure to face the problem. This usually occurs when the problem has not been properly defined.
2. Mistaking goals for strategy. This was the mistake made by Lehman Brothers.
3. Bad strategic objectives. Beware a long list of objectives that are not prioritized or even connected to one another.
4. The final hallmark is what Rumelt calls "fluff," or hubris. Distrust a strategy that restates the obvious with buzzwords. Rumelt gives the example of a retail bank that proclaimed: "Our fundamental strategy is one of customer-centric intermediation." In reality, intermediation is banking. *Customer-centric* was meaningless. So once the buzzwords were removed, the bank's strategy boiled down to being a bank—tautological at best.

Proceed with caution but nevertheless proceed.

Notes

Chapter 1

1. Markides, Costas, "Fine-Tuning Your Strategic Thinking," *Business Strategy Review*, 12, no. 3, 2001.
2. All unattributed quotations are from author interviews.
3. Hughes, Daniel (ed.), *Moltke on the Art of War*, Presidio Press, 1993.
4. Sun Tzu, *The Art of War* (trans. Griffiths), Oxford University Press, 1963.
5. Ibid.
6. Machiavelli, Niccolò, *The Prince*, Penguin, 1967.
7. Von Clausewitz, Carl, *On War*, Princeton University Press, 1976 (revised ed. 1984).
8. Kiechel, Walter, *The Lords of Strategy: The Secret History of the New Corporate World*, Harvard Business School Press, 2010.

9. Ansoff, H. I., "A Profile of Intellectual Growth," in *Management Laureates*, A. G. Bedeian (ed.), JAI Press, 1994.

10. Ansoff, H. I., *Strategic Management*, Macmillan, 1979.

11. Ansoff, H. I., *New Corporate Strategy*, Wiley, 1989.

12. Kiechel, Walter, *The Lords of Strategy: The Secret History of the New Corporate World*, Harvard Business School Press, 2010.

13. "Professor Porter PhD," *Economist*.

Chapter 2

1. Porter, Michael, *Competitive Strategy*, Free Press, 1980.

2. Ibid.

3. Porter, Michael, "How Competitive Forces Shape Strategy," *Harvard Business Review*, March 1979.

4. Porter, Michael, *Competitive Strategy*, Free Press, 1980.

5. Ibid.

Chapter 3

1. Wernerfelt, Birger, "A Resource-Based View of the Firm," *Strategic Management Journal*, 1984.

2. Byrne, John, "Three of the Busiest New Strategists," *Businessweek*, August 26, 1996.

3. Hamel, Gary, and Prahalad, C. K., *Competing for the Future*, Harvard University Press, 1994.

4. Ibid.

5. Learned, Edmund Philip, Christensen, C. Roland, Andrews, Kenneth, and Guth, William D., *Business Policy: Text and Cases*, Irwin, 1965.

6. Hamel, Gary, and Heene, Aime (eds.), *Competence-Based Competition*, Wiley, 1995.

7. Hamel, Gary, and Prahalad, C. K., *Competing for the Future*, Harvard University Press, 1994.

8. Prahalad topped the Thinkers50 ranking in 2007 and 2009.

Chapter 4

1. D'Aveni, Richard, *Hypercompetition*, Free Press, 1994.
2. Ibid.
3. D'Aveni, Richard, "Corporate Spheres of Influence," *MIT Sloan Management Review*, Summer 2004.
4. D'Aveni, Richard, "Spheres of Influence: Constructing a Forcefield to Deflect Competitors," *Financial Times*, August 16, 2002.
5. D'Aveni, Richard, "Corporate Spheres of Influence," *MIT Sloan Management Review*, Summer 2004.

Chapter 6

1. Mintzberg, Henry, "Five Ps for Strategy," *California Management Review*, June 1987.
2. Mintzberg, Henry, *The Rise and Fall of Strategic Planning*, Prentice-Hall, 1994.
3. Ahlstrand, Bruce, Lampel, Joseph, and Mintzberg, Henry, *Strategy Safari*, 2d ed., Prentice-Hall, 2008.

Chapter 8

1. A group of companies with interlocking business relationships and shareholdings.
2. Each major bank was part of a *zaibatsu* group of companies before World War II. As part of a *zaibatsu*, each firm owned parts of other group firms, and each acted with the others to compete against other *zaibatsu*. The occupational government formally broke up the *zaibatsu* after the war, but the big banks still act as central bankers for several companies that often bear the bank's name.

Acknowledgments

We would like to thank Steve Coomber for his help with this book. We are grateful to our Thinkers50 colleagues Joan Bigham and Deb Harrity for their essential and creative contributions. We would also like to thank all the people we have interviewed over the last 20 years writing about business thinking, in particular, David Bach, Richard D'Aveni, Pankaj Ghemawat, Gary Hamel, W. Chan Kim, Rita McGrath, Roger Martin, Renée Mauborgne, Henry Mintzberg, and Chris Zook. We especially would like to acknowledge the intellectual generosity of the late C. K. Prahalad.

Index

About the
Authors

Adjunct professors at IE Business School in Madrid, Stuart Crainer and Des Dearlove create and champion business ideas. They are the creators of Thinkers50 (www.thinkers50 .com), the original global ranking of business thought leaders. Their work in this area led *Management Today* to describe them as "market makers par excellence."

As journalists and commentators, Stuart and Des have been asking difficult questions for more than two decades. Now, they help leaders come up with their own wicked questions and explore how best to engage with people and communicate the answers. They were advisors to the 2009 British government report on employee engagement, and associates of the Management Innovation Lab at London Business School.

Their clients include Swarovski, the Department of Economic Development in Abu Dhabi, Fujitsu, and Heidrick & Struggles.

Stuart and Des have been columnists at the *Times* (London), contributing editors to the American magazine *Strategy+Business*, and edited the bestselling *Financial Times Handbook of Management*. Their books include *The Management Century, Gravy Training, The Future of Leadership*, and *Generation Entrepreneur*. These books are available in more than 20 languages.

Stuart is editor of *Business Strategy Review*. According to *Personnel Today*, he is one of the most influential figures in British people management. Des is an associate fellow of Saïd Business School at Oxford University and is the author of a bestselling study on the leadership style of Richard Branson.

Des and Stuart have taught MBA students, professors, and senior executives in programs all over the world. These include the Oxford Strategic Leadership Programme at the Saïd Business School at Oxford University; Columbia Business School in New York; the Tuck Business School at Dartmouth College in New Hampshire; IMD in Lausanne, Switzerland; and London Business School.

About the Thinkers50

The Thinkers50, the definitive global ranking of management thinkers, scans, ranks, and shares management ideas. It was the brainchild of Stuart Crainer and Des Dearlove, two business journalists, who identified a place in the market for an independent ranking of the top management thinkers. First published in 2001, the Thinkers50 has been published every two years since.

In 2011, Crainer and Dearlove added a number of award categories and hosted the first ever Thinkers50 Summit, described as "the Oscars of Management Thinking." The 2011 winner was Harvard Business School's Professor Clayton Christensen. The previous winners were C. K. Prahalad (2009 and 2007), Michael Porter (2005), and Peter Drucker (2003 and 2001).

The ranking is based on voting at the Thinkers50 website and input from a team of advisors led by Stuart Crainer and Des Dearlove. The Thinkers50 has 10 established criteria by which thinkers are evaluated:

- Originality of ideas
- Practicality of ideas
- Presentation style
- Written communication
- Loyalty of followers
- Business sense
- International outlook
- Rigor of research
- Impact of ideas
- Power to inspire

Business strategies from
THE WORLD'S MOST ELITE BUSINESS THINKERS

Available in print and eBook